To Dave

With Best Wishes!

[signature]

"When pondering meditatively cloud banks in the sky, one might yet be surprised when a fellow observer draws alongside and points out intriguing formations that one had not noticed. So might one respond to the third in the Davenport-Lloyd trilogy on US politics, *How Public Policy Became War*. They have pinpointed habits of thought and expression that meaningfully illuminate contemporary discourse. In doing so they vindicate their observation that 'if we learn nothing else from the American Founding, it is that in the end it is the character of the people and the quality of the institutions that are the keys to the success or failure of the American experiment.'"

> —**W. B. Allen**, *Dean Emeritus, James Madison College, and Emeritus Professor of Political Science, Michigan State University*

"F. A. Hayek famously described how the market order (catallaxy) expands the boundaries of human society by turning strangers into friends, or at least trading partners. In their exploration of the expanding treatment of public policy as war, David Davenport and Gordon Lloyd help us to understand how modern politics and 'statesmanship' has worked in the opposite direction, diminishing society by turning our neighbors into potential enemies. The war metaphor shapes the very ways we can deliberate about public problems and ultimately pits us against nature and the constraints of our own humanity. This book offers timely insight and a call to citizens to disarm and work together to improve the institutions of self-governance."

> —**Lenore T. Ealy**, *Secretary and Executive Director, The Philadelphia Society*

"David Davenport and Gordon Lloyd see 1933 as the year that 'changed everything,' and not least the language of governing. They trace the phases by which war became our default mode, not only for elections but for the policy making in between. Both penetrating and persuasive, they show how this mind-set has undermined the deliberation Congress was once imagined to provide. The authors also remember to offer ideas for restoring the legislative process to health and to the function the founders intended."

> —**Ron Elving**, *NPR News, and Professor, American University School of Public Affairs*

[continued next page]

"The American constitutional order was designed, as James Madison told us, so that the 'cool and deliberate sense of the community' might prevail in our political life. This book is written in the spirit of Madisonian deliberation and provides an important antidote to the warlike atmosphere that has too often prevailed in Washington for some four score and seven years."

— **Christopher Flannery**, *Executive Director, The Ashbrook Center at Ashland University*

"Metaphors matter, especially in a democracy, because they are the carriers of large and consequential ideas. As David Davenport and Gordon Lloyd demonstrate in this crisp and compelling study, the United States has paid an enormous price for our reflexive resort to the word 'war' to describe any and all important government actions. Its promiscuous use has gone hand in hand with the cultivation of a constant state of national emergency and the creation of a veritable army of crises that can never be allowed to go to waste. It has provided essential support for the steady growth of the administrative state, and has greatly contributed to the decline of our discourse and to the enervation of our capacity for democratic deliberation. It is time to kick the habit, give peace a chance, and entertain other and better metaphors to galvanize and guide our actions."

— **Wilfred M. McClay**, *University of Oklahoma*

"Ideas have consequences in politics and policy, but so do words in shaping public opinion. In this important book, Davenport and Lloyd invite us to consider how the word 'war' has been used by public leaders to effectively quash deliberative policy making on an array of issues—foreign and domestic. In this polarized era, Davenport and Lloyd's concern about political rhetoric is more important now than ever."

— **Pete Peterson**, *Dean, Pepperdine School of Public Policy*

How
Public
Policy
Became
War

How Public Policy Became War

DAVID DAVENPORT AND
GORDON LLOYD

HOOVER INSTITUTION PRESS

STANFORD UNIVERSITY   STANFORD, CALIFORNIA

With its eminent scholars and world-renowned library and archives, the Hoover Institution seeks to improve the human condition by advancing ideas that promote economic opportunity and prosperity, while securing and safeguarding peace for America and all mankind. The views expressed in its publications are entirely those of the authors and do not necessarily reflect the views of the staff, officers, or Board of Overseers of the Hoover Institution.

www.hoover.org

Hoover Institution Press Publication No. 700

Hoover Institution at Leland Stanford Junior University, Stanford, California 94305-6003

Copyright © 2019 by the Board of Trustees of the Leland Stanford Junior University

First printing 2019

25 24 23 22 21 20 19   7 6 5 4 3 2 1

Manufactured in the United States of America

The paper used in this publication meets the minimum Requirements of the American National Standard for Information Sciences—Permanence of Paper for Printed Library Materials, ANSI/NISO Z39.48-1992. ♾

Cataloging-in-Publication Data is available from the Library of Congress.

ISBN: 978-0-8179-2264-1 (cloth. : alk. paper)
ISBN: 978-0-8179-2266-5 (epub)
ISBN: 978-0-8179-2267-2 (mobi)
ISBN: 978-0-8179-2268-9 (PDF)

Contents

Introduction . . . 1

 The War Metaphor
in Public Policy . . . 5

 How Public Policy Became
"Action, and Action Now" . . . 25
THE NEW DEAL

 How Public Policy Became
War and Emergency . . . 57
THE MODERN PRESIDENCY

 What Public Policy Was
Supposed to Be . . . 93
DELIBERATION AT THE FOUNDING

 How to Manage the War
Metaphor in Public Policy . . . 121
THE WAY FORWARD

About the Authors . . . 158
Index . . . 159

Introduction

Any way you look at it, 1933 was an important year. Globally, Adolf Hitler became chancellor of Germany and opened the Nazis' first concentration camp, at Dachau. At home, a major drought in the Midwest created a Dust Bowl that pushed families into new migration patterns across the country. The Great Depression hit its worst year, with one in four Americans out of work. Franklin D. Roosevelt replaced Herbert Hoover as president and immediately closed the banks in an effort to stem a panic of cash withdrawals. The first one hundred days of Roosevelt's New Deal in 1933 ushered in the most revolutionary set of domestic policies in American history. In an apocalyptic message, Roosevelt proclaimed, "the mechanics of civilization came to a dead end" in March 1933.

This is now our third book that grows from the soil of 1933. We have come to believe that 1933 was not just an important year, but was also a turning point, a hinge on which history turned. In our first book together, *The New Deal and Modern*

American Conservatism: A Defining Rivalry (Stanford, CA: Hoover Institution Press, 2013), we claim that both modern American conservatism and liberalism were born in 1933 with the launch of the New Deal, which we believe was America's French Revolution, changing everything. In our view, the New Deal versus modern American conservatism was the defining rivalry of the 1930s but also today, and we can better appreciate and participate in today's policy debates by understanding that.

In our second book, *Rugged Individualism: Dead or Alive?* (Stanford, CA: Hoover Institution Press, 2017), we found Herbert Hoover's "rugged individual" and Franklin Roosevelt's "forgotten man" confronting one another in 1933. Rugged individualism, a term coined by Herbert Hoover in his 1928 presidential campaign, and described more fully in his 1921 essay "American Individualism," was used to describe American exceptionalism following World War I, in contrast to the several brands of totalitarianism in Europe, where Hoover had been working. Hoover's rugged individualism lost at the ballot box to Franklin Roosevelt in 1932, and progressives launched an all-out attack on it beginning in 1933 and continuing today. Rugged individualism has been caricatured as a myth at best, and devil-take-the-hindmost laissez-faire economics (today called "income inequality") at the worst. But rugged individualism did not die in the hearts of many Americans over these seventy-five years of repeated intellectual and political assaults.

Now, in this book, we claim that 1933 is the year that the war metaphor staked its claim on American public policy in a way that has grown to epic proportions today. We remember the assuring words in Roosevelt's first inaugural address, "All we have to fear is fear itself." Far more important, however, if less memorable, was his statement of the role of the federal government in general and of the presidency in particular. What the American people need and demand, Roosevelt said in that same address, is "action, and action now." We must stand together, under the president's leadership, as a disciplined army ready to do battle against this new enemy, the Great Depression. In a radical departure from the way the US government had worked since its founding, major policies were to be initiated by the president, not Congress, and run by a new and growing administrative state. If Congress did not support this sweeping set of changes, Roosevelt indicated he would ask Congress for war powers to accomplish what was needed. Roosevelt's speeches and actions, we claim, brought the war metaphor forward as the new normal in American public policy, replacing the slower, steadier, deliberative approach created by the Founders in 1787.

By now, presidents have declared war on a whole set of domestic problems: wars on poverty, crime, drugs, terror, energy consumption, and the like. America also lives currently under twenty-eight states of national emergency, again declared by presidents. Public policy has literally become a war in America, both in its goals and objectives and in the manner by which it is developed and carried out. After tracing these developments over the past seventy-five years, we close with a brief exploration of where we might go from here, looking especially at what

Congress might do, but also what the American people must do to better manage the war metaphor in public policy today. We have come to believe that the future of our republic depends on our ability to do this.

 —David Davenport, *Stanford, California*
  Gordon Lloyd, *Malibu, California*
  October 2018

1 The War Metaphor In Public Policy

America is at war. As the longtime "world's policeman," engaged now for nearly two decades in a global war on terror, it is not surprising that we are fighting wars literally all over the world. Global politics in the late twentieth century were characterized as a "cold war." Even economic policies such as the imposition of tariffs on imported goods are understood as having launched a "trade war" among nations.

More surprising, however, is that we are also in a state of war at home. Presidents, most obviously beginning with Lyndon Johnson in the 1960s, have declared wars that continue to this day on a host of domestic problems: poverty, crime, drugs, and terror, to name a few. War's close cousin, the national emergency, has also become a way of doing policy business in the United States. Few Americans realize that they currently live under twenty-eight states of national emergency, many declared decades ago.

Living in a constant state of domestic war and national emergency has dramatically changed the way public policy is made and conducted in America. In our view, this is neither accidental nor good. Presidents have discovered that declaring wars and emergencies is a way of grasping greater executive power at the expense of Congress. Rather than engaging in long-term policy development and debate, presidents can take over a field of domestic policy essentially through speeches and declarations of domestic war. Such wars seemingly never end, since all the domestic wars, beginning with Lyndon Johnson's War on Poverty in 1963, are still in effect.[1]

The war metaphor itself is a powerful rhetorical tool that has shaped domestic policy. There are troops to muster, enemies to fight, and battles to win. There is little time and opportunity for policy deliberation because, after all, we are at war. In war, the president becomes commander in chief and domestic policies shift from the leadership of Congress to the White House. Few domestic problems are ever finally solved, so a war on this or that challenge becomes, in effect, a permanent frame for how to deal with issues such as poverty, crime, or drugs. It is not too much to say that our leaders in Washington, DC, have fully embraced the war metaphor, so much so that deliberation—which the Founders saw as the key to policy formation—has largely given way to action, emergency, and war.

The effect of constant war in the policy world was described well by fictional president Jonathan Duncan in Bill Clinton and James Patterson's 2018 novel *The President Is Missing*: "There is no trust anymore. In the current environment there's no gain in it. All the incentives push people in the opposite directions." Duncan then described "the real cost of this," namely "more frustration, polarization, paralysis, bad decisions and missed opportunities." President Duncan lamented that "everybody knows it's wrong" yet we continue, "assuming that our Constitution, our public institutions, and the rule of law can endure each new assault doing permanent damage to our freedoms and way of life."[2] Unfortunately, the war metaphor is not limited to the world of fiction; the damage it causes is real.

The War Metaphor

Metaphors not only communicate ideas but also help shape them. To say that something is like another thing is to conjure up known images to understand something new or different. We use these figures of speech all the time to give fuller and more colorful expression to ideas we seek to convey: we say that certain words are "music to our ears," that a danger is "a train wreck waiting to happen," but after the problem is over there will be "clear skies." Metaphors are everywhere.

In particular, metaphors have become important in the realm of policy and politics. In a more objective sense, metaphors are useful to help people who may not engage regularly in policy debates and discussions to understand the nuances of public policy. A picture, as they say, is worth a thousand words. In immigration policy, for example, we used to think about America as a "melting pot," with people from many cultures blending, but more recently, it has been described as a "salad bowl," with groups maintaining their own identity inside the larger society. Politicians sometimes run for office by promoting "wedge issues" such as abortion to energize a base of voters on one side or the other of the wedge. Our government is prone to "pork barrel politics" and "mudslinging" while we wait for Donald Trump to "drain the swamp" or some new "dark horse" candidate to rise up and rescue us.

Less well understood is that policy metaphors not only help citizens understand nuances of policy, but they are also used to persuade audiences in one direction or another, and they may ultimately result in setting limits and making choices about policy itself. George Lakoff and Mark Johnson, in their foundational book *Metaphors We Live By*, note that, as a starting point, metaphors "play a central role in the construction of social and political reality."[3] Policy metaphors are more than descriptive—they are building blocks toward a certain kind of policy. In their article on metaphors in health policy, Mark Schlesinger and Richard R. Lau rightly point out that reasoning based upon policy metaphors takes place in two distinct stages: "the first descriptive and the second prescriptive."[4] Policy metaphors start out describing and amplifying, but they soon end up defining, limiting, and proposing solutions.

Of several lenses—economic, political, sociological—through which we could look at public policy since the Great Depression, the war metaphor has become pervasive and describes much of what has been going on. When we declare war on a domestic policy problem, as presidents from Franklin Roosevelt to Lyndon Johnson and beyond have been inclined to do, all kinds of things—from the descriptive to the persuasive and ultimately the prescriptive—take place. The war metaphor is the strongest possible figure of speech because of its ability to marshal a following and focus a policy agenda. Yet, as Professor Jeremy Elkins has noted, "[T]he war model . . . deserves more attention than it has received."[5]

A president's declaration of war on a domestic issue—be it poverty, crime, or drugs—is initially an exercise of the president's bully pulpit. President Theodore Roosevelt coined that term to describe the powerful platform available to a president to focus energy and attention on issues. In his day, the term "bully" was less about force or leverage, as it might be understood today, and simply implied a wonderful or fabulous opportunity for a president to draw attention to issues of importance. With modern tools of communication—from fireside radio chats in FDR's day to the cool medium of television for the telegenic John F. Kennedy, to the great communicator and speech maker Ronald Reagan, and now to Donald Trump's tweets—the rhetorical power of the president to influence events has become increasingly important, and this is the launching point for presidential declarations of domestic war.

One wonders whether a president would find constitutional authority for the declaration of a war on poverty or crime. When the Constitution was drafted, a war meant quite literally a war against foreign enemies, and the power to make that formal declaration was granted to Congress under Article I, Section 8. The president, as commander in chief, was empowered to carry out the wars that Congress declared. One might debate whether, by analogy, the power to declare war on a domestic enemy should also be reserved to Congress, but presidents have simply asserted the power and, since initially it is largely a rhetorical device, such declarations have not been challenged. Ultimately, as we shall see, far more than rhetoric is committed to such wars, so the question of the role of Congress is one that needs more careful consideration.

First and foremost, a declaration of war on a domestic enemy has the effect of rallying the troops—both those inside and outside the Beltway—into a focused attack on a policy problem. Franklin Roosevelt said in his first inaugural address that the American people wanted "action, and action now" to tackle the Great Depression, and through his powerful rhetoric, energized leadership, and far-reaching New Deal policies, he gave them just that. In his 1964 State of the Union message, President Lyndon B. Johnson declared "an unconditional war on poverty" that would seek to "cure it" and "above all to prevent it." This declaration of war kicked off the extensive legislative agenda of "the Great Society," as Johnson called it, changing American economic and domestic policy to this day. Presidents from Richard Nixon on have sought to rally the American people and the Congress into wars on crime and drugs. President Jimmy Carter sought a similar outcome when he declared "the moral equivalent of war" on energy consumption, but with less effect.

It is important to note that even at this initial rhetorical level, a declaration of war begins to change the making of domestic policy. First, the president seizes the initiative: this is his program, his initiative in which he hopes to engage the efforts and support of Congress and the American people. And as we shall see in greater detail, the president engages the topic not at the nuanced level of concrete policy proposals, but at the broader "all hands on deck" level, with the greater emotional commitment of a war. The declaration of a war on drugs or crime is thus more of a political strategy than it is a set of policy prescriptions. The American people ought to get behind the war effort, and Congress needs to allocate funds for it. As the columnist Prospero rightly put it in *The Economist*, "War . . . focuses attention: there is no greater national emergency. War calls for urgency, unity and sacrifice. Leaders in wartime can expect a singleness of purpose from their followers that no other situation can command."[6]

As the war rhetoric becomes more elaborate, its effect moves from the motivational to the descriptive and even the prescriptive. At its most basic level, a declaration of war changes the conversation. No longer are lawmakers examining the policy nuances and choices presented by complex problems such as poverty or drugs; instead we are moving into immediate action and war. The question becomes not so much what we should do about it and more about how to amass the money and energy to do something. As will be seen in the following chapters, Franklin Roosevelt was not committed to this or that policy on many issues, but instead was focused on "bold, persistent experimentation" leading to "action, and action now." Lyndon Johnson gathered his staff a month or so before his famous war on poverty address and told them he would carve out money for the effort and that they should figure out how to spend it. With antipoverty policy little understood or developed, his advisers came back with a proposed series of small experiments. Having little patience for small policies, Johnson instead declared an

11

open-ended war with very little policy to implement it. This is typical of how these domestic wars begin: long on rhetoric and short on policy.

The specifics of the war rhetoric, then, begin to shape the policy, not vice versa. Wars need enemies and weapons. Generals and czars must be commissioned to lead them. Battlefields are identified, tactics developed, and victory defined. All of this is in marked contrast with the kind of analytical and deliberative work that should attend the development of public policy. Indeed, there is a sense that there is little time or space for working up and debating policy alternatives because, after all, we are at war! When Jimmy Carter declared "the moral equivalent of war" on energy consumption, he transformed this domestic challenge into a matter of national security as he called for sacrifices and spoke of imposing sanctions. The war on drugs quickly transformed our nation's schools into literal battlegrounds over drugs. The war on crime brought military equipment into our nation's cities and police forces. Without question, declaring war on a domestic problem dramatically transforms both the way policy is made and how it is carried out.

One of the trickiest elements of the war metaphor revolves around the question of who is the enemy. Many were puzzled when President George W. Bush declared war on terrorism in a televised speech a few days after 9/11, characterizing it in a subsequent message to Congress as a war on terror. How does one engage in a war on a methodology, not against a nation or a traditional enemy? But a similar dilemma is raised by other domestic policy wars that seem to be wars on abstractions or conditions, not enemies per se. Poverty, drug use, energy consumption, crime—these are all conditions or problems, not enemies in a personalized sense. Can you really declare a war on a condition? If you do, will it inevitably turn into a war against some people—drug dealers, criminals—and is there some danger that even victims of poverty or drug use may come to feel like enemies in the war?

Another important question is why presidents have employed the war metaphor in domestic policy in the first place. Clearly, a large part of a president's agenda is mobilizing support and action. FDR drew on the recent experience of World War I in proposing a warlike campaign on the Great Depression. Lyndon Johnson was in search of an issue he could call his own (as opposed to merely finishing John F. Kennedy's legacy) and a cornerstone for the Great Society when he declared war on poverty. Barack Obama used the war metaphor following an oil spill to try to mobilize support for his stalled environmental and energy agendas.

But another reason for declaring war on domestic problems is consolidating greater power in the presidency itself. Under the Constitution, health and welfare (underpinnings of poverty), crime, and the like are all matters of state and local control, not federal. Other than directing the work of administrative agencies, Congress retains jurisdiction over federal domestic policy, especially through its oversight and spending powers. By declaring war on a domestic problem, however, a president seizes not only the initiative but also the power to drive policy from the White House. Even when he needs approval from Congress, the president goes to the Hill with a declared war, not just a set of policy options. There is little doubt that power-savvy presidents such as Franklin Roosevelt, Lyndon Johnson, and Richard Nixon understood this very well and that increasing presidential power was not only an outcome of declaring domestic policy wars but was also very much part of their intention. So the incentive for presidents to declare policy wars is high indeed.

Problems with the War Metaphor

At first blush, one might think that declaring war on intransigent problems such as poverty or crime would be a good thing. As these domestic policy wars have evolved, however, five conclusions become relatively clear: (1) they do not generally solve the problem at hand; (2) they create roadblocks to better policy solutions; (3) they increase executive power at the expense of Congress; (4) their imagery is often negative and destructive; and (5) they never end. In a larger sense, these domestic policy wars also contribute to the contentious policy and culture wars that have plagued Washington in recent years.

A declaration of war on a domestic policy issue is flawed from the outset because it oversimplifies the problem, precluding further debate and the discovery of better solutions. To declare war is to state that, in effect, we understand the problem and we are prepared to do what it takes to eradicate or solve it. Such a declaration necessarily oversimplifies the problem in order to focus and attack, which is the methodology of war. When a president takes a very complex problem—such as poverty, crime, drug use, terrorism, energy—and suggests that we understand it and know how to eradicate it by declaring a war, the process of study, deliberation, and consideration of alternatives is essentially over. We are now in the context of war, where the operative approach is action, not deliberation. As Lori Hartmann-Mahmud has written of the war metaphor: "Clearly, the metaphor of war applied to concepts such as poverty, drug abuse, over-population and terrorism simplifies and thus misleads."[7]

If we look at the historical record, however, presidents were not able to say they understood a complex domestic problem and the necessary solutions when they declared war, and more likely were launching a marketing or political campaign that was long on rhetoric and money but short on policy and solutions. Johnson's war on poverty was developed in a month to be featured in his first State of the Union message as president. The wars on crime and drugs were primarily about federalizing battles and spending more money on problems that had overwhelmed state and local governments. Much more policy work was needed in every case, however, that was inhibited by the declaration of war. There was no time to study and identify root causes of the problems or consider alternative solutions. As Lakoff and Johnson point out in their book on metaphors, such devices inherently clarify one aspect of a problem while keeping us "from focusing on other aspects . . . that are inconsistent with that metaphor."[8]

In short, the war metaphor focuses policy too quickly and narrowly, preventing lawmakers from considering alternatives.

Should the war on drugs focus primarily on limiting supply or reducing demand, for example? These complex and nuanced questions are difficult to debate once we appoint a czar for drug policy and go to war against the problem. Indeed, Hartmann-Mahmud rightly points out that such complexities "are not readily addressed in a theater of war."[9] Another observer adds that a policy metaphor can "so limit our vision that any other approach becomes unthinkable, unimaginable."[10] The very strengths of the war metaphor—action, speed, narrow focus—are enemies of deliberation and policy development.

A further problem created by the war metaphor is that such wars are never finally won, leaving the country in a perpetual state of war. If you consider the primary domestic policy wars declared since LBJ's war on poverty in 1964, they are all still under way. Neither poverty, nor crime, nor drugs, nor terror, nor energy consumption has been defeated, so we fight on, adding new fronts to the domestic policy wars as we go. Since most of these wars span several administrative departments and agencies, no one is tasked with reviewing or reorganizing the war policies, much less sunsetting them or declaring an end of hostilities. Wars over some of society's most complex problems are simply unwinnable and, therefore, never-ending.

In addition, domestic wars have the harmful effect of shifting the balance of power between Congress on the one hand and the executive branch on the other. All of these domestic policy wars have been declared by presidents—from Johnson to Nixon to Carter, Reagan, and George W. Bush—and not by Congress. If it is consulted at all, Congress is merely called upon to authorize spending more money for the wars, but even this step is organized and advanced by the president. Further, because there is no single budgetary line item for a war on poverty or crime or terror, the actual costs of the war are buried in dozens of agency and program budgets, making it even more difficult for Congress to exercise its power of the purse and oversight. As a result, a domestic war becomes yet one more tool at a president's disposal to increase his power, to launch new initiatives, and to leave a legacy for posterity.

The cumulative effect of twenty-eight national states of emergency under which the country now lives, plus at least half a dozen major domestic wars, is powerful and widespread. Congress is supposed to review the national states of emergency regularly, but it does not. It seems equally important for Congress to review a long-term war—such as that on poverty or crime or drugs—but again that kind of oversight is difficult when presidents declare and sustain these wars on their own authority. If each president going forward were to add one domestic policy war and a few national emergencies to the agenda, soon much of domestic policy would be without any process of review and nearly beyond the reach of Congress.

Finally, we note that war is a term of destruction, given to negative connotations of attacking and defeating enemies. If we are constantly at war, America becomes a nation under siege. Perhaps the initial idea of declaring war on a major problem such as poverty or crime has a moment of optimism, but that soon gives way to the destructive tactics and drawn-out nature of a war. It is hardly the kind of metaphor one would want for a nation's public policy compared with more positive possibilities that have been part of our history such as John Kennedy's new frontiers or Ronald Reagan's city on a hill. American exceptionalism, a more positive image, has itself become a subject of war. In the war metaphor, we have settled for an organizing idea that is negative, destructive, and discouraging, whereas we would be better served by metaphors of hope and optimism.

Just Win, Baby

The war metaphor has already captured much of domestic policy and has become a primary way of doing business in Washington, DC. In part, these wars develop because of intractable problems that presidents would like to solve, and they believe an all-out war might uncover some new approach or in some way overwhelm the challenges that state or local governments, or even the federal government, has not been able to do. Presidents also turn to wars to grow executive power over new fields of public policy, enabling them to carry out Franklin Roosevelt's admonition during the Great Depression for "action, and action now" rather than follow the slow, deliberative process of working things through Congress.

Yet another reason why wars, emergencies, and action have overtaken deliberation and compromise is the devolution of policy into a political game with a singular focus on winning. Policy was never devoid of politics, but historically politics came to the fore during campaigns for office and then government leaders settled into the more collaborative process of legislating, with the regular exercise of committee hearings and debates, the consideration of amendments, and resulting compromises. When Ronald Reagan was president and Tip O'Neill Speaker of the House, one saw this sort of process at work, with Reagan once advising O'Neill that he would accept half a loaf today, but would return for the other half. Even though O'Neill and Reagan had very different worldviews, they carefully cultivated the sort of personal and professional relationship that would allow them to work through problems on behalf of the country.

Today the policy arena has become an extension of the political game of campaigning and the new mantra we would borrow from Al Davis, the late owner of the Oakland Raiders: "Just win, baby." Legislators rarely develop relationships with colleagues from the other party, but instead stay within their own party caucus. To the extent that other groups of legislators are formed, there are even narrower interest groups within a party (the Tea Party caucus or Freedom Caucus, for example), rather than bipartisan groups between the parties. If bipartisan groups are formed now, they are characterized by the pejorative term "the gang," as in the gang of seven or the gang of nine coming together to try to work something through. Party discipline—delivering the votes of your party—is now at a premium, since we often pass important legislation on a purely party-line vote. Rather than compromise, now legislators threaten to shut down the government if they do not get their way. Often the mere threat of a shutdown moves Washington onto a war footing.

Congressional expert David Mayhew has observed that winning the next election would always be important, perhaps the highest priority, for a member of Congress.[11] This has been taken to new highs—or lows—in Washington today. Difficult votes are avoided altogether if they might cause a member to lose ground for reelection. Bills are held by the party leadership, often in secret, until enough party-line votes are available for sure passage. Recalcitrant members may be threatened by the possibility of the party supporting an opponent in their next primary election. There is very little allowance for compromise and, unless absolutely necessary, for reaching out to members of the other party. The power in Congress has shifted from committee chairs to majority and minority leaders, who are essentially leaders of their political party. All of this has added up to heightened polarization in Washington and an atmosphere of gridlock and political warfare, not deliberation and compromise to achieve the best policies for the good of all the people.

Managing the War Metaphor

In all likelihood, the war metaphor in domestic policy and politics is here to stay for the foreseeable future. It would be nice to think that some new president, or a different set of leaders in Congress, would decide to quit governing by means of wars, emergencies, and polarized conflict. If one takes the pendular view of history, in which things swing in one direction, then hit some kind of wall and start swinging back, it is at least theoretically possible that Washington wars would hit some kind of voter backlash or policy wall and start back toward deliberation and collaboration. But there is no sign of that now.

It may be helpful to recognize that the war metaphor has, in a sense, always been with us. The Founders, neither naive nor utopian, realized that "faction"—the capacity to be warlike—was sown in the nature of man. As James Madison said in *Federalist* No. 10, we could do away with faction but only by doing away with liberty. In ancient times, Plato's republic did away with liberty to avoid the warring tensions between the ideal and the practical, between the higher and lower worlds. So we would not propose giving up liberty to avoid war.

There are several reasons why the war metaphor continues to resonate in Washington. If we think about its coming to the fore under Franklin Roosevelt and the New Deal, some of those conditions still exist. In large part, Roosevelt turned toward the war metaphor because of the deep-seated emergency of the Great Depression and the American people's clamor for, as Roosevelt put it, "action, and action now." Although American domestic policy faces nothing like the disaster of the Great Depression, politicians nevertheless create a constant sense of crisis, whether it is immigration and the nation's borders, or tariffs on imported goods that trigger a trade war, or climate change necessitating new environmental policies, and there are always urgent matters that seemingly require action. Presidents have learned that a sense of crisis or emergency is actually helpful in their moving forward with a domestic agenda, so there is little reason to think that will end anytime soon.

Additionally, Roosevelt moved toward war and emergency to extend presidential power and transform not only domestic policy but also the presidency itself. Roosevelt saw Congress as too slow to deal with emergencies, so it was incumbent on him and his executive agencies to take on more and more responsibility. Beginning with Roosevelt, then, and extending through both Republican and Democratic presidents, there has been steady growth in the accumulation and use of executive power, whether through executive orders, declarations of war and national emergency, extending the president's war powers, growing the role of the administrative state, and so on. Power in Washington has been traveling a one-way street down Pennsylvania Avenue from the Capitol to the White House for decades. We have yet to see a president in modern times who would voluntarily see that end.

With these underlying dynamics and motivations toward war and emergency, it seems more realistic to manage the war metaphor rather than expect Washington to give it up entirely, and to put other metaphors and forces into play to help balance it. In chapter 5 we suggest several ways of managing and supplementing the war metaphor with reference to Plato's "divided line." Above our divided line, we propose that Congress must claw back powers it has ceded to the executive branch and become once again more deliberative. Below the line—where we, the people live—there is a great need for civic education and participation.

We focus heavily on the need to clean and strengthen filters at the line between the people and their government. The

Founders did not establish a direct democracy, but rather a representative government—as Benjamin Franklin put it, "a republic, if you can keep it." Because faction is sown in the nature of man, the Founders established all manner of filters that let the good things through and stop the bad. Filters cleanse, remove impurities, and interpose a medium between the people and their government. They are a mechanism to cool the passions of the people, as George Washington described the effect of drinking hot coffee out of a saucer. Many of those filters have become clogged and no longer serve their purpose. Restoring and reactivating those filters is a key to managing and minimizing the war metaphor and returning to more positive and deliberative metaphors for public policy in America today.

NOTES

1. Although the President's Council of Economic Advisers declared in July 2018 that the War on Poverty was "largely over and a success," we have doubts about that. See David Davenport, "Foolhardy Presidents Keep Declaring 'War' on Problems They Can't Solve," *Washington Examiner*, July 24, 2018, https://www.washingtonexaminer.com/opinion/foolhardy-presidents-keep-declaring-war-on-problems-they-cant-solve.

2. Bill Clinton and James Patterson, *The President Is Missing* (New York: Little, Brown and Co., 2018), 59–60.

3. George Lakoff and Mark Johnson, *Metaphors We Live By* (Chicago: University of Chicago Press, 1980), 159.

4. Mark Schlesinger and Richard R. Lau, "The Meaning and Measure of Policy Metaphors," *American Political Science Review* (September 2000): 613.

5. Jeremy Elkins, "The Model of War," *Political Theory* 38, issue 2 (2010): 214.

6. Prospero by R.L.G., "The War Metaphor," *The Economist*, August 1, 2017.

7. Lori Hartmann-Mahmud, "War as Metaphor," *Peace Review* (2002): 430.

8. Lakoff and Johnson, *Metaphors We Live By*, 10.

9. Hartmann-Mahmud, "War as Metaphor," 429.

10. Rebecca Gordon, "No, We Don't Need a 'War' on Domestic Issues," *The Nation*, August 15, 2017.

11. David R. Mayhew, *Congress: The Electoral Connection* (New Haven, CT: Yale University Press, 1974), 13, 36–37.

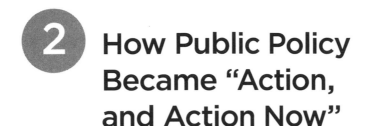

2 How Public Policy Became "Action, and Action Now"

THE NEW DEAL

"Action, and Action Now"

President Barack Obama's chief of staff, Rahm Emanuel, could well have been describing President Franklin D. Roosevelt and his New Deal when he said, "You never want a serious crisis to go to waste. . . . [It's] the opportunity to do things that you could not do before."[1] Coming into office at the height of the Great Depression, Roosevelt declared an emergency, moving domestic and economic policy onto an emergency war footing. But he did not stop with short-term responses to the emergency, continuing his campaign of "action, and action now" to accomplish longer-term changes to the American system, implementing his New Deal progressive policies, and strengthening the presidency at the expense of Congress. The New Deal became, in effect, America's French Revolution, creating a permanent change in both what government does and how it does it.

No one would deny that the Great Depression constituted a crisis. At the time of Roosevelt's inauguration in March 1933, thirteen million Americans were unemployed, leaving about one-fourth of the workforce seeking jobs. National income had been reduced by half. Thousands of banks had closed, with twenty-five states declaring bank holidays. Addressing the resulting crisis of confidence and morale in the nation, Roosevelt famously said in his first inaugural address, "The only thing we have to fear is fear itself."

However, the phrase in that speech that most accurately pointed the path Roosevelt would take as president was, "This nation asks for action, and action now." Columbia University economist Rexford Tugwell, who was part of the president's "brain trust," said of Roosevelt, "He did not very much care *what kind* of farm relief, or *how* the principle of cheap and universally available power was arrived at. Banking regulations might be of any practicable sort, and the methods used for relieving the unemployed were open to argument. But he was committed to *some* action in all these matters."[2] Roosevelt's preference for government action over deliberation led the way to a permanent change in how Washington, DC, works.

The Progressive Path to the New Deal

Although Franklin Roosevelt was the right man and the Great Depression was the right moment for launching a revolution in American public policy, many of the ideas on which the New

Deal was built had been developing for decades. The rise of progressivism in the late nineteenth and early twentieth centuries was foundational, as four strands of thought came together in the New Deal: Frederick Jackson Turner, his "frontier thesis" and the closing of the American western frontier; Charles Beard and his "myth of American rugged individualism"; Theodore Roosevelt and his emphasis on national government and the Progressive Party platform; and Woodrow Wilson with his studies of administration and the importance of experts in government. Of particular importance to our study are Theodore Roosevelt's nationalism and Woodrow Wilson's work on the administrative state.

A political movement in search of a candidate to personify its vision landed upon Theodore Roosevelt, who, having served as a Republican president from 1901 to 1909, ran again for the presidency in 1912 as the candidate of the Progressive Party. Many of his progressive ideas were expressed in a 1910 speech, "The New Nationalism," which argued for a fundamental change in the role of the national government with respect to the private sector. All problems were now national problems, in Roosevelt's view, and especially the problematic relationship between capital and labor. Rather than leave regulation of wealth to markets, individuals, or the state and local governments, this should be the province of the federal government, in Roosevelt's view.

Finally, there is Woodrow Wilson with his progressive ideas of replacing the political spoils system with expert administrators. Underlying his thinking was the notion that it was possible, and desirable, to distinguish the dirty realm of congressional politics from the enlightened science of executive administration.[3] Wilson later argued that Americans spent too much time worrying over constitutional niceties and whether the president was becoming too strong, when they should stay out of the details of government and stop being meddlesome.[4] As our society became more complex and industrial, Wilson argued that we needed more expert administration and fewer citizens trying to run things through the corrupt and self-interested political process.

A "Return to Normalcy"?

While these progressive ideas laid the groundwork for a major change in the American system, and specifically a dramatic expansion of the role of the national government in regulating economic and social affairs, three Republican presidents of the 1920s sought to lead in a very different direction. Following the rise of federal government power during World War I, Warren G. Harding ran for the presidency in 1920 urging a "return to normalcy." In his campaign speech of that title, Harding said, "all human ills are not curable by legislation" and the "quantity of statutory enactment and excess of government offer no substitute for quality of citizenship." He noted that the "problems of maintained civilization are not to be solved by a transfer of responsibility from citizenship to government." In stark contrast to Franklin Roosevelt's later call to put American economic and domestic policy on a war footing, Harding said America needed to "get out of the fevered delirium of war" and called forth the "normal forward stride of all the American people."

When Harding died in office in 1923, Vice President Calvin Coolidge assumed the presidency, and he continued the effort to move America away from its wartime approach. In particular, Coolidge worked diligently, and in painstaking detail, to trim the federal budget back to pre–World War I levels. Herbert Hoover followed as president in 1929, advocating for what he called the American system of rugged individualism, accompanied by equality of opportunity. Having lived and worked in Europe during and following World War I, Hoover could not understand why America would be tempted to give in to the several kinds of totalitarianism that were overtaking the Continent.

These two strands of thought were in conflict, especially during the postwar era of the 1920s. On one hand, the progressives saw America as a new industrialized country needing new forms of progressive, national, and executive leadership, especially in the regulation of the economy and in establishing social justice. Meanwhile, Republican presidents of the 1920s called for a return to normalcy, moving away from the wartime centralization of power in Washington and the outsized federal budget.

Developing and advocating a new philosophy of government started the progressives' project, but completing it required the right moment and the right leader. Finally, in the Great Depression, progressives seized their moment, and in Franklin Roosevelt they discovered their leader. Under Roosevelt's leadership, progressives found the opportunity not just to respond to the economic emergency of the Great Depression, but also to completely remake American domestic and economic policy for the next eighty years (and still counting). Moreover, in the process they would reset the balance of power away from Congress and the states and toward a strong president and executive branch, while also shifting the federal government away from deliberation toward war and action.

Roosevelt Laid the Rhetorical Base for a Domestic War

Certainly compared with "Silent Cal" Coolidge and dour Herbert Hoover before him, Franklin Roosevelt was a master communicator. His frequent speeches and press conferences, along with his novel fireside chats to the nation on radio, pioneered many tools of communication that are now part and parcel of the modern presidency. A review of Roosevelt's speeches during the campaign and early in his presidency plainly conveys his deliberate attempt to marshal the tools of war, emergency, and action he deployed in his presidency.

During the campaign for the presidency in 1932, for example, in Roosevelt's "forgotten man" message of April 7, he said it was "high time to admit with courage that we are in the midst of an emergency at least equal to that of war. Let us mobilize to meet it." In his speech accepting the Democratic Party's nomination for president on July 2, 1932, he claimed that this was "more than a presidential campaign, it is a call to arms." In his address on long-range planning on October 31, 1932, Roosevelt complained that the president "cannot get action from Congress. . . . He cannot get things done," noting that, by contrast, he would "pledge action to make things better."

No speech better exemplifies Roosevelt's move away from deliberation to action and war than his first inaugural address, delivered on March 4, 1933. Although his most famous line from the speech is "the only thing we have to fear is fear itself," his most prophetic line was "This nation asks for action, and action now." He indicated that the federal government needed to get behind this action, "treating the task as we would treat the emergency of a war." Contrary to the American founding of limited government and deliberation, Roosevelt instead called for "discipline," claiming, "We must move as a trained and loyal army willing to sacrifice for the good of a common discipline," without which "no progress is made, no leadership becomes effective."

Roosevelt invoked the precedent of World War I to ground his case for a war at home. When signing the National Industrial Recovery Act on June 16, 1933, he referred to "the great cooperation of 1917 and 1918," expressing his "faith that we can count on our industry once more to join . . . to lift this new threat." He viewed the act itself as "the most important of this kind in history," adding that as in "the great crisis of the world war, it puts a whole people to the simple but vital test: 'Must we go on in many groping, disorganized, separate units to defeat or shall we move as one great team to victory?' "[5] We agree with historian William H. Leuchtenburg that World War I dramatically grew the powers of the federal government and the role of the administrative state in a way that progressives admired, and Roosevelt sought to carry that forward into domestic governance in the New Deal.[6]

The rhetoric of war continued through Roosevelt's presidency, leading right up to the next major war, World War II. In a fireside chat on July 24, 1933, for example, Roosevelt called upon employers to launch "a great summer offensive against unemployment." He sent a wire to a small-town Oklahoma chamber of commerce, saying, "The public will be asked to renew its war time patriotism and support only those who join in this program."[7] In a 1936 speech accepting his nomination for another term as president, Roosevelt said, "Here in America we are waging a great and successful war," noting that he was "enlisted for the duration of the war." In a later fireside chat on April 14, 1938, Roosevelt spoke of the need for Americans to be armed with three rounds of ammunition to beat the crisis.

To those who might have been concerned about a limited federal government or the need for deliberation, Roosevelt said in his first inaugural address that all this action "is feasible under the form of government which we have inherited from our ancestors." Laying the groundwork for his idea of a living Constitution, Roosevelt said, "Our Constitution is so simple and practical that it is possible always to meet extraordinary needs by changes in emphasis and arrangement without loss in essential form." The people do not care so much about formal democracy as they do "essential democracy" and that preference has been registered by their vote for president, which Roosevelt called a "mandate that they want direct, vigorous action."

While Roosevelt "hoped that the normal balance of executive and legislative authority may be wholly adequate to meet the unprecedented task before us," if "undelayed action" is required, then we may have to depart from normal "public procedure." Furthermore, he added, if Congress does not respond to his proposals to combat the national emergency, he will "ask Congress for the one remaining instrument to meet the crisis . . . broad executive power to wage a war against the emergency, as great as the power that would be given to me if we were in fact invaded by a foreign foe."

By contrast, when Herbert Hoover delivered his presidential nomination address in 1928, he noted that World War 1 "released ideas of government in conflict with our principles." The role of the federal government had expanded in World War 1 such that if things continued in that way, "the ideal of individualism based upon equality of opportunity" would be altered. But according to Roosevelt, we were now in another Great War, this one at home. And the people had spoken. By electing him their president, they wanted action, not deliberation, and action now. Roosevelt meant to take up all the powers necessary to deliver action, laying the groundwork through his rhetoric of war, emergency, and action.

The Emperor of Executive Orders

Presidents have issued executive orders throughout history, either to direct one of the executive departments to act in a particular way or to carry out a responsibility assigned to the president by Congress in legislation. But no president had used executive orders as broadly as did Franklin Roosevelt, not only to tackle the emergency of the Great Depression but also to jump-start the revolutionary policies of his own New Deal. For a president promising "action, and action now," executive orders became tools of choice.

Roosevelt's first executive order, establishing a national bank holiday, set the tone for the president's willingness to establish policy through executive action rather than deliberation. President Herbert Hoover had considered declaring such a holiday to stabilize the banking crisis, but he would have been troubled by both the federal intervention into the economy and the question of a president's constitutional authority to do so. But these questions did not bother Roosevelt, who went to work on the matter on his first day in office and, by the following day, established a national bank holiday by executive order.

On the question of constitutional authority for an executive order closing the banks, influential senator Carter Glass insisted the president was not permitted to do so.[8] But Roosevelt's advisers began poring through old statutes from World War I and discovered one—the Trading with the Enemy Act of 1917—that had been designed to prevent gold from reaching enemy nations, but that might be stretched to cover the situation at hand. There was even a question whether the law might, through various amendments, have been repealed. Legal opinions on the matter were divided, but Roosevelt chose to act based upon its authority, and a nationwide bank holiday was declared.[9] Action, and action now! The *New York Times* called the president's order the "most drastic" exercise of presidential power "ever taken in peacetime to safeguard the nation."[10] Eric Rauchway rightly noted that this established the president's pattern of leadership, taking "swift action of sometimes dubious constitutionality."[11]

In terms of sheer numbers, Roosevelt set the record for the most executive orders signed by a president, at 3,721. The next in line, Woodrow Wilson, had only half as many (1,803). By contrast, our modern presidents are mere slackers, with George W. Bush at 291 and Barack Obama with 277.[12] But to understand the scope of Roosevelt's executive orders, one must look behind the quantity to the quality. His executive orders went far beyond the routine, to fundamental actions that one would logically think should have been the subject of deliberation and legislative action.

For example, in 1939, Roosevelt established the Executive Office of the President, the foundation of the modern presidency, by executive order.[13] In 1933 alone, when Roosevelt was establishing his leadership, he reformed the farm credit agencies, started up the revolutionary Civilian Conservation Corps, regulated gold, increased the powers of federal agencies, closed and reopened the banks, and so on. No one had seen anything like it before or since. It was all part of the revolution that Roosevelt led in domestic and economic policy, largely through executive action.

When Roosevelt did go to Congress, he often came away with broader executive authority arising out of legislation that he carried out through additional executive orders. For example, the National Industrial Recovery Act (NIRA) empowered the president to establish codes of fair competition that would govern wages, work weeks, and other aspects of a variety of industries. Ultimately, the Supreme Court held that this was an unconstitutional delegation of Congress's power to the executive branch.[14] However, as scholars Bruce P. Frohnen and George W. Carey point out in their recent book, "This decision, potentially limiting presidential power, has been allowed to atrophy as the administrative state has grown in size and complexity."[15] In that sense, even Roosevelt's thwarted initiatives had the long-term effect of growing executive power.

Roosevelt's broad and extensive use of executive powers provides an insight into his understanding of presidential leadership. Whereas executive orders had generally been a grant of some flexibility by Congress to the president in executing legislation without returning constantly for greater or more specific authority, Roosevelt used executive orders in the first instance to take initiative. It was as though the leadership he felt was needed could not wait on Congress even to originate legislation. This was a sharp contrast from the leadership notions of Roosevelt's predecessor, Herbert Hoover, whose approach was one of cooperative government, bringing people together for discussion, but not for action, not for the drafting of laws or issuing of orders. Roosevelt's broad use of executive orders across so many topics had the effect of moving things steadily from the table of congressional deliberation to the desk of the president.

Riding Congress "Like a Skilled Jockey"

Although Roosevelt established himself as the master of executive orders, it was largely his unprecedented leadership of Congress that put the federal government firmly on a domestic emergency footing. Whereas previously Congress had carefully maintained its status as a separate branch from the executive, drafting and deliberating over its own legislation, it became virtually an extension of Roosevelt's presidency, especially during the first hundred days of the new president's term. Historian David Kennedy described it when he concluded that, in the early days of the New Deal, "Roosevelt had ridden the Congress like a skilled jockey, the staccato whip-touches of his several brief, urgent messages stirring the balky House and Senate to unprecedented movement."[16]

Roosevelt foreshadowed his bold approach with Congress in his first inaugural address, saying he would ask Congress to give him "broad executive power to wage a war against the emergency, as great as the power that would be given to me if we were in fact invaded by a foreign foe." And, only five days after his inauguration, Congress came into a special session with an urgent message from the new president: "I cannot too strongly urge upon the Congress the clear necessity for immediate action."[17] From that point forward, Congress was subjected to what historian Arthur Schlesinger has called "a presidential barrage of ideas and programs unlike anything known to American history."[18]

The pattern of Roosevelt driving the legislative agenda was set with the passage of the banking regulations in the first days of the New Deal. Roosevelt had already issued an executive order closing the banks and immediately sent Congress a bill to strengthen federal regulation of the banks, which was itself a bold change in the relationship between the government and the economy. The legislation was hammered together in the early morning hours before it was sent to Congress and was, as one historian noted, "jammed through a frightened Congress which knew little of its contents."[19] According to Arthur Schlesinger's account, Congress was so pressed by Roosevelt's sense of urgency that the chairman of the Banking and Currency Committee "read aloud the only available copy of the proposed banking legislation," debate was limited to forty minutes, and the same afternoon, "the House passed unanimously and without a roll call the bill few of its members had ever seen."[20]

The dramatic shift in power from Congress to the executive continued with the passage of the National Industrial Recovery Act; the Agriculture Adjustment Act; and, in just the first hundred days, a total of fifteen major laws. The way these laws were enacted constituted a shift away from legislative deliberation to executive action. In his recent book, historian Ira Katznelson points out that this kind of emergency presidential leadership was unusual in three ways: (1) the executive branch drafted the bills, not Congress; (2) debate was cut short, amendments were barred, and legislative consideration was highly abbreviated;

and (3) huge powers were delegated by the bills to the executive branch and its growing number of federal agencies.[21]

Roosevelt used several tools at his disposal to lead and cajole Congress. He held meetings with party leaders and invested considerable time—by his own estimate three to four hours per day—in his office and on the telephone persuading members to go along.[22] He exercised the presidential veto power over a broad number of measures.[23] From the opening message to Congress to proposed drafts of legislation, from phone calls and meetings twisting arms to pressing for rapid action, and vetoing what he did not like, Roosevelt exercised unprecedented presidential leadership over what was supposed to be a structurally separate and coequal branch of government.

Roosevelt was so successful riding Congress like a skilled jockey that he persuaded congressional leaders to extend the special session. In these additional days, he presented Congress with measures that went beyond the emergency and began to lay the groundwork for the larger New Deal. When the special session was over, Roosevelt had sent fifteen messages to Congress and had signed fifteen bills into law. As presidential historian Clinton Rossiter rightly observed, in so doing he had launched "an unvarnished crisis government" that shifted many powers from Congress to the White House.[24]

We agree with historian William H. Leuchtenburg who argues that Roosevelt developed "the role of chief legislator . . . to an unprecedented extent."[25] In the first hundred days especially, Roosevelt drafted bills, lobbied members of Congress for their approval, and initiated the practice of making the signing of bills a major event, with presidential pens for bill sponsors. Author and journalist Godfrey Hodgson observed that Congress in those first hundred days "did not so much debate the bills it passed . . . as salute them as they went sailing by."[26] Progressives have admired the British parliamentary system, and columnist Raymond Clapper wrote in 1937 that it is "scarcely an exaggeration to say that the President, although not a member of Congress, has become almost the equivalent of the prime minister of the British system, because he is both executive and the guiding hand of the legislative branch."[27]

Of course, his work with Congress continued beyond the first hundred days. Two years into his presidency, Roosevelt was still seeking emergency action, calling on Congress in his January 4, 1935, State of the Union message to authorize the creation of 3.5 million "emergency jobs" for those who were still unemployed. In his State of the Union message to Congress the following year, on January 3, 1936, Roosevelt continued to speak of the "battle" in which he was engaged to fight back against the forces of "entrenched greed" and the "unscrupulous money-changers." This was, Roosevelt said, a struggle for power in the new order as the economic titans used their "weapon of fear." The president invited his opponents to come to Congress and seek a vote if they felt they had better approaches to the crisis in the land. That would have been difficult to accomplish when the president continued his leadership through both executive power and his skillful command of Congress.

Removing Constitutional Barriers

With his executive power pen inked up, and Congress willingly following his lead, Roosevelt faced one final barrier to his plan to exercise vast executive powers: the Constitution. In his first inaugural address, Roosevelt sought to preempt any concern that the Constitution, with its checks and balances and separations of powers, would get in the way of his aggressive agenda. He described the Constitution as "so simple and practical that it is possible always to meet extraordinary needs by changes in emphasis and arrangement without loss of essential form." In other words, brace yourselves for some serious constitutional reinterpretation. And, he added, if that is not sufficient, "I shall ask the Congress for the one remaining instrument to meet the crisis—broad executive power to wage a war against the emergency." Roosevelt moved on both of these fronts—constitutional reinterpretation and engaging Congress as his partner—to avoid constitutional limits and barriers to his New Deal set forth in the Constitution. Whereas the Founders saw the Constitution as both an empowering and a restraining document (see chapter 4), Roosevelt drew from its power and overlooked its restraints.

Franklin Roosevelt's reinterpretation of the Constitution laid the groundwork for what would later become known as the "living Constitution" school of understanding our founding document. Especially in his speech on the 150th anniversary of the signing of the Constitution, delivered on September 17, 1937,

Roosevelt laid out his case for a broad, flexible, and evolving understanding of the Constitution. As a starting point, Roosevelt argued that the Constitution, as drafted, was "a layman's document, not a lawyer's contract," a point that he added "cannot be stressed too often." This was important to Roosevelt because it provided a basis for his claim that in broad matters such as "the fundamental powers of the new national government," sufficiently wide latitude is provided in the document so that it could "adapt to time and circumstance." Clearly he was attacking those who would question his expanding powers and thereby, as he warned, "shrivel the Constitution into a lawyer's contract."

Roosevelt also drew upon the first words of the Constitution, "We the people," to avoid barriers to his project. He pointed out that "the overwhelming majority of the American people fully understand and completely approve . . . the course of the present government of the United States." Invoking the sense of emergency or crisis, Roosevelt recited a litany of earlier changes that took courts or other government entities twenty years to enact, concluding that the country could "no longer afford the luxury of twenty-year lags." Clearly, the president was ready to override the separation of powers and checks and balances and simply say that if "We, the people" demand change, the Constitution empowers me to carry out that change. Specifically Roosevelt found in "the great mass of our people" an "insistence" in favor of higher living standards and social justice.

As the president pushed proposed legislation through Congress, the bills often contained broad delegations of power to the executive branch. *Time* magazine reported that the Agriculture

Adjustment Act delegated powers to the president "so broad that few could see their limits."[28] Congressman Fred Britten of Illinois said it was "more Bolshevistic than any law or regulation existing in Soviet Russia," while Representative Joseph W. Martin of Massachusetts declared that the country was "on our way to Moscow."[29] Such claims were also made about the National Industrial Recovery Act (NIRA) and many others as well. Indeed, in the case of the NIRA, the Supreme Court held the delegations of power from Congress to the president to create and approve a wide range of industrial codes and policies to be unconstitutional in the famous case of *A.L.A. Schechter Poultry Corp. v. United States* in 1935,[30] and similarly found the Agriculture Adjustment Act unconstitutional in *United States v. Butler* in 1936.[31]

The Supreme Court's action prompted Roosevelt to attack directly the separation of powers among the branches well established in the Constitution with his famous analogy of horses pulling a wagon. In his March 9, 1937, fireside chat, Roosevelt told the American people that the courts had "cast doubts on the ability of the elected Congress to protect us against catastrophe by meeting squarely our modern social and economic conditions." He went on to describe the American system as three horses—the three branches, executive, legislative, and judicial—pulling the wagon so that the American field might be plowed, noting, however, that while "two horses were pulling in unison, one was not." The branches, he said in his September 17, 1937, speech, needed to be "interdependent" as well as independent. Attacking what we would call today judicial activism, Roosevelt argued that the Supreme Court has "improperly set itself up as a third house of the Congress" reading things into the Constitution. This sort of presidential critique of the Court would be viewed today as a direct and inappropriate attack on the independence of the judiciary and the separation of powers.

Roosevelt's solution, as he said in that same fireside chat, was to inject some "new and younger blood" into the Court by adding a new justice whenever a current justice reached the age of seventy and did not retire. Although the president claimed there was "nothing new or radical" about this idea, most did not agree with him, calling it a blatantly political effort to "pack the Court." Although Roosevelt's Court-packing plan failed, he nevertheless won the judicial war when the Supreme Court itself began, with the minimum wage law, to uphold the president's legislative agenda.[32] All three horses were now pulling toward a permanent delegation of power to the president and executive branch. Journalist Ernest Lindley rightly concluded that Roosevelt was "endowed with greater power than any American had possessed in peace-time since the adoption of the Constitution," through a revolution "within the framework of democratic institutions."[33]

Building Out the Modern Presidency

Although the New Deal policies may have begun as a response to the economic emergency of the Great Depression, Roosevelt did far more than address the immediate crisis. In the end, he greatly expanded and radically transformed the role of the federal government. Within the federal government itself, he also effected a major change by shifting power from the more deliberative bodies in Congress to the executive branch and ultimately to the White House itself. Rather than debating economic policies in the House and Senate, there is the enduring image of Roosevelt in his morning bedclothes deciding where to peg the price of gold for the day.[34] It is no exaggeration to say that Franklin Roosevelt created the powerful modern presidency.

Prior to Roosevelt, the federal government had been relatively small. But federal spending more than tripled between 1930 (under Herbert Hoover) and 1940 (in Roosevelt's second term). In the first six years of Roosevelt's presidency, federal employment grew by nearly 60 percent, from 572,000 to 920,000.[35] Roosevelt created scores of new government agencies and commissions—approximately forty in his first year alone—preferring to assign powers to newly formed agencies rather than the old executive departments. Instead of returning to prewar levels after World War II, the federal government continued to grow in size and scope.

To consolidate his power, Roosevelt created the Executive Office of the President in 1939, establishing a platform for the modern presidency that continues to this day. Roosevelt shepherded the Executive Reorganization Act through Congress and then followed up by executive order to create the basic machinery of an enlarged White House office and operation. He also strengthened the Bureau of the Budget and generally consolidated executive power in the president.

A key component of Roosevelt's building out of the modern presidency was the importance of central planning and expert administrators, which he saw as superior to the political processes of Congress as well as the vagaries of free markets. As Roosevelt said in his bold Commonwealth Club speech in San Francisco on September 23, 1932, "The day of the great promoter is over" and the "day of enlightened administration has arrived." No longer could we trust executives and free markets to oversee the economy, but the federal government, and especially the executive branch, needed to step in. His secretary of the interior, Harold Ickes, described this breathtaking set of changes in his book *The New Democracy*:

> Wise and comprehensive planning on a national scale fits into the social vision of the future. If, as I believe, we are now definitely committed to the testing of new social values; if we have turned our backs for all time on the dreadful implications in the expression "rugged individualism"; if we have not given over the care and custody of ourselves and our children to the tender mercies of an outworn and ruthless social order; if it is our purpose to make industrialism serve humanity instead of laying ourselves as victims on the cruel order of industrialism, then national planning will become a major government activity.[36]

This was the vision that drove the creation of new agencies to regulate the economy.

An additional factor in consolidating power in the modern presidency was the growing public appreciation of the president, over Congress and the political parties, as the true political leader of the nation. One important element in this development, according to Sidney M. Milkis, was the implementation by many states of the direct primary in the early twentieth century, affording the president an opportunity to appeal directly to the people over the heads of parties and their congressman.[37] Then, too, Roosevelt's fireside chats and personalized communication enhanced his standing as a leader of all the people, even more so than one's own congressman. This was not the role envisioned by the Founders, since they saw the legislature as the first and most powerful branch, so it was an important shift in constitutional practice. And it was all accomplished without any constitutional amendments or even reinterpretations. It was a shift in perception first, and then of power.

To truly comprehend the scope and impact of the New Deal, however, one must add (or even multiply) the combined effects of the economic crisis, Roosevelt's own personality, the growth in power and size of the federal government, the shift of power from the legislative to the executive branch, and Roosevelt's New Deal policies. All told, this constitutes nothing less than a revolution in the function, power, and operation of the federal government. From a relatively small and restrained government of the 1920s, Roosevelt grew a large and active federal government, led by a robust modern presidency, with a much more expansive view of what government should do, and with a mandate for "action, and action now."

We have described Roosevelt's New Deal elsewhere as America's French Revolution, a transformation that coalesced modern American conservatism as its eighty-year (and still counting) rival.[38] We are not alone in making this claim.[39] Journalist and author Adam Cohen acknowledged bluntly that the "Roosevelt revolution created modern America."[40] Political scientists Sidney Milkis and Jerome Mileur were even more specific: "[T]he New Deal took the shape of a 'regime' that marked a critical departure in the governing principles, institutional arrangements, and policies that shaped American political life." We agree (see chapter 3) with their description of later developments, such as the Great Society of the 1960s, as "an extension rather than a departure from the New Deal regime."[41] As historian Ira Katznelson said in his more recent account of the New Deal, it "reconsidered and rebuilt the country's long-established political order."[42]

Of particular concern to our story, however, about how public policy became a revolutionary war and not a deliberative project, is that Roosevelt managed to shift power from the more deliberative body, the US Congress, to the action-oriented executive branch. And by creating an emergency footing, calling forth metaphors of war and action, Roosevelt created an environment in which deliberation was no longer welcome or needed. The questions about agriculture and industry were no longer whether it was appropriate for the federal government to act, or even which policies made the most sense; rather the order of the day was "action, and action now." As presidential historian Clinton Rossiter recalled, Roosevelt launched "an unvarnished crisis government" that shifted powers from Congress to the

White House.[43] Unfortunately, this revolution effected a permanent change, and both the New Deal and the proactive modern presidency remain with us as legacies of the Roosevelt years.

Roosevelt's Second Inaugural Address: Capturing the Gains

Franklin Roosevelt's second inaugural address, on January 20, 1937, was clearly aimed at capturing the gains in power and policy of the first four years and turning them into a permanent mode of governance. Roosevelt reminded his audience that, at the time of his first inaugural, the country was full of anxiety and that the government had moved into "action, tireless and unafraid" to overcome the "stagnation and despair of that day." And we did this, he said, by using government as the "instrument of our united purpose to solve for the individual the ever-rising problems of a complex civilization." Prior attempts to solve them without government, he added, "had left us baffled and bewildered." We needed government to restore order.

All of this new government oversight was entirely constitutional, Roosevelt argued, foreshadowing his battles with the Supreme Court over shifts of power from Congress to the president. And we must keep going, he said. We cannot stop with just a "patchwork job" but rather we need to complete "a new order of things." We have not reached the promised land, Roosevelt observed, so we must keep going. He saw "one third of a nation ill housed, ill clad, and ill nourished." No longer is government limited to addressing disasters and problems, but it must now "solve problems once considered unsolvable." We must "secure the blessings of liberty to the American people," Roosevelt said, quoting the preamble to the Constitution. To do so, Roosevelt sought to fashion "an instrument of unimagined power."

Roosevelt saw that the real challenge to liberty was social injustice and that it was the role of the federal government to solve that. His agenda was no longer equality of opportunity, which he had said was now dead, but rather equality of outcome. Roosevelt rightly said, in his second inaugural address, that he was "writing a new chapter in our book of self-government . . . using new materials of social justice." It was time, Roosevelt thought, to use government as a tool to create greater economic equality and social justice. This speech was a harbinger of things to come, with a growing federal government dedicated to the cause of social justice, often at the expense of individual liberty.

We have elsewhere recounted how Roosevelt's government crusade for social justice has undermined American individualism.[44] Roosevelt's argument was that rugged individualism had worked only for the wealthy and that both greater government regulation of the economy and increased government assistance for the "forgotten man" were needed to balance the scales. Harold Ickes, Roosevelt's secretary of the interior, said we had "turned our backs for all time on the dreadful implications in the expression 'rugged individualism,'"[45] and progressive thinker John Dewey referred to it as "ragged individualism."[46] The debate between progressives who favor social justice and collectivism and conservatives who champion individual liberty continues to this day, but the New Deal definitely tipped the scales away from individualism and toward government control.

Roosevelt's Limited Opposition: The Emergency Never Ended

There was really only one persistent opponent to Roosevelt's revolution: Herbert Hoover. We have described Hoover elsewhere as a voice crying in the wilderness throughout the 1930s, pointing out the excesses of the New Deal.[47] Sometimes referred to as a progressive himself, Hoover was shocked by the scope of the New Deal, referring to it variously as "a challenge to liberty" and "economic regimentation." Hoover biographer George Nash has edited a lost manuscript of Hoover's writing about the New Deal called *The Crusade Years*, which aptly describes Hoover's tireless speeches and writing against the revolutionary New Deal.[48] While Hoover's critique of the New Deal laid the philosophical groundwork for modern American conservatism of the 1950s and beyond, in the wake of the Great Depression and the perception of Hoover's failure as president to deal with it, his arguments gained little traction during the New Deal itself.

The New Deal crisis was soon replaced by the emergency of World War II, after which there was no return to normalcy for the federal government with its increased size and enhanced powers. When Barack Obama was elected president in 2008, a *Time* magazine cover showed Obama with Roosevelt's top hat and long cigarette, proclaiming "A New New Deal" as a way of describing his programs. In 2015, the US Supreme Court held that a New Deal relic, the Raisin Administrative Committee, could not take a California farmer's raisins in violation of the Fifth Amendment "takings" clause of the Constitution.[49] So the New Deal lives on, as does the paradigm of emergency administrative action by the executive branch, rather than deliberation in Congress.

The Postwar Era Cemented the New Deal Paradigm

With no return to normalcy following the extraordinary New Deal and World War II, presidents from 1945 to 1963 essentially made the New Deal paradigm permanent. A return to normalcy had been called for by Warren Harding after World War I, and was actively pursued by presidents Calvin Coolidge and Herbert Hoover throughout the 1920s. But, alas, postwar presidents Truman, Eisenhower, and Kennedy, from the late 1940s to the early 1960s, continued to build on the rhetoric of war and an emphasis on executive power and action.

President Truman, for example, broke new ground with his executive order for the secretary of commerce to seize and operate most of the country's steel mills in 1952. President Eisenhower, himself a major war leader, appeared to be influenced by the war metaphor and growth in executive power in domestic policy, building the interstate highway system and creating the Department of Health, Education, and Welfare as a cabinet-level department. President John F. Kennedy argued for greater urgency and "vigor" in government generally, calling for a New Frontier and winning the race to space ahead of the Soviets. Most of Kennedy's domestic policy agenda was cut short by his assassination less than three years into office, but he had teed up several key policy proposals that his successor, Lyndon Johnson, would use to remake domestic policy in a broad, sweeping, and warlike way.

NOTES

1. Gerald F. Seib, "In Crisis, Opportunity for Obama," *Wall Street Journal*, November 21, 2008, http://www.wsj.com/articles/SB122721278056345271.

2. Adam Cohen, *Nothing to Fear: FDR's Inner Circle and the Hundred Days That Created Modern America* (New York: Penguin Press, 2009), 6.

3. Woodrow Wilson, "The Study of Administration," *Political Science Quarterly* 2, no. 2 (June 1887): 197–222.

4. Woodrow Wilson, *Constitutional Government in the United States* (New York: Columbia University Press, 1908).

5. See Wilfred M. McClay, "The Moral Equivalent of War?," *National Affairs* (Fall 2010).

6. William H. Leuchtenburg, *The FDR Years* (New York: Columbia University Press, 1995), 74–75.

7. Ibid., 59.

8. Adam Cohen, *Nothing to Fear,* 68.

9. Ernest K. Lindley, *The Roosevelt Revolution* (New York: Viking Press, 1933), 78.

10. Ibid., note 3, 73.

11. Eric Rauchway, *The Great Depression and the New Deal: A Very Short Introduction* (New York: Oxford University Press, 2008), 57–58.

12. "Executive Orders," The American Presidency Project, http://www.presidency.ucsb.edu/data/orders.php, accessed October 10, 2017.

13. Kenneth R. Mayer, *With the Stroke of a Pen: Executive Orders and Presidential Power* (Princeton, NJ: Princeton University Press, 2001), 5.

14. A.L.A Schechter Poultry Corp. v. United States, 295 U.S. 495, 529 (1935).

15. Bruce P. Frohnen and George W. Carey, *Constitutional Morality and the Rise of Quasi-Law* (Cambridge, MA: Harvard University Press, 2016), 207.

16. David M. Kennedy, *Freedom from Fear* (New York: Oxford University Press, 1999), 149.

17. Arthur M. Schlesinger, Jr., *The Coming of the New Deal* (Boston: Houghton Mifflin Co., 1958), 7.

18. Ibid., 20–21.

19. Ernest K. Lindley, *The Roosevelt Revolution* (New York: Viking Press, 1933), 71.

20. Schlesinger, *The Coming of the New Deal*, 7.

21. Ira Katznelson, *Fear Itself: The New Deal and the Origins of Our Time* (New York: Liveright Publishing Corp., 2012), 95.

22. Schlesinger, *The Coming of the New Deal*, 554.

23. Ibid., 555. See also Leuchtenburg, *The FDR Years*, 18.

24. Clinton L. Rossiter, *Constitutional Dictatorship: Crisis Government in the Modern Democracies* (Princeton, NJ: Princeton University Press, 1948), 257–58.

25. Leuchtenburg, *The FDR Years*, 16.

26. Godfrey Hodgson, *All Things to All Men: The False Promise of the Modern Presidency* (New York: Simon and Schuster, 1980), 60.

27. Raymond Clapper, "Resentment Against the Supreme Court," *Review of Reviews* (January 1937): 38.

28. "Untrod Path," *Time*, March 27, 1933, 13.

29. Schlesinger, *The Coming of the New Deal,* 40.

30. 296 U.S. 495 (1935).

31. 297 U.S. 1 (1936).

32. Amity Shlaes, *The Forgotten Man* (New York: HarperCollins, 2007), 308, 315.

33. Lindley, *The Roosevelt Revolution*, 4–5.

34. Shlaes, *The Forgotten Man*, 147.

35. Katznelson, *Fear Itself*, 36.

36. Harold L. Ickes, *The New Democracy* (New York: W. W. Norton, 1934), 120–21.

37. Sidney M. Milkis, "Franklin D. Roosevelt, the Economic Constitutional Order, and the New Politics of Presidential Leadership," in *The New Deal and the Triumph of Liberalis,* ed. Sidney M. Milkis and Jerome M. Mileur (Boston: University of Massachusetts Press, 2002), 44–45.

38. Gordon Lloyd and David Davenport, *The New Deal and Modern American Conservatism: A Defining Rivalry* (Stanford, CA: Hoover Institution Press, 2003), 2.

39. See, e.g., Katznelson, *Fear Itself*, 9.

40. Cohen, *Nothing to Fear*, 11.

41. Milkis and Mileur, *The New Deal and the Triumph of Liberalism*, 2.

42. Katznelson, *Fear Itself*, 9, 11.

43. Rossiter, *Constitutional Dictatorship*, 257–58.

44. David Davenport and Gordon Lloyd, *Rugged Individualism: Dead or Alive?* (Stanford, CA: Hoover Institution Press, 2017).

45. Harold L. Ickes, *The New Democracy,* 120–21.

46. John Dewey, *Individualism Old and New* (New York: Minton, Balch, 1930), 18.

47. Lloyd and Davenport, *The New Deal and Modern American Conservatism.*

48. George Nash, ed., *The Crusade Years, 1933–1955* (Stanford, CA: Hoover Institution Press, 2013).

49. Horne v. Department of Agriculture, 135 S. Ct. 2419 (2015).

3 How Public Policy Became War and Emergency

THE MODERN PRESIDENCY

The story of the modern era of the federal government, from World War II and the New Deal to the twenty-first century, is a narrative of replacing deliberative politics with the politics of action, emergency, and war. As a consequence, it is also a story about the rise of the president and the executive branch over Congress and the states. These developments cannot be plotted on a straight-line trajectory, but rather unfold in fits and starts. The trend line, however, is clear: the federal government has come to value Franklin Roosevelt's "action, and action now" while devaluing deliberation, and the executive branch is now clearly in the driver's seat in Washington, not Congress. These trends do not bode well for American democracy (see chapter 5) and are clearly at odds with the Founders' understanding of the republic (see chapter 4).

To some degree the story is one of presidents building on Roosevelt's game plan to grow presidential powers and increase government action, with the acquiescence of Congress. This incremental narrative sees presidents following the Roosevelt playbook: laying the rhetorical base, increasing the use of executive orders, riding Congress "like a skilled jockey," removing constitutional barriers, and building out the modern presidency (see chapter 2).

But there were also more dramatic developments to the story during the modern era of presidents (1964–2018): the invention of the domestic war, the flow of the president's war powers over into domestic policy, and the further rise of executive power in response to hyperpartisanship and government gridlock. Taken together, these three developments significantly increased the federal government's field of play, generated "action, and action now," and grew the president's own span of control. And these wars and emergencies, with their resulting increase in presidential power, took on a kind of permanence, as most of them are still being waged today, decades after their launch.

Domestic Wars

The War on Poverty

The first case of declaring a war on a domestic policy problem is Lyndon Johnson's "war on poverty," announced in his first State of the Union message, on January 8, 1964. Johnson's hero Franklin Roosevelt made generous use of the war metaphor in tackling the Great Depression, but in this case Johnson employed it to initiate a new domestic priority. In the early days of his presidency, Johnson knew he wanted to complete Kennedy's policy legacy, but he also sought an issue of his own to champion. Eliminating poverty became that cause.

Why a "war" on poverty rather than merely a program? The record on this is not entirely clear. The early thinking among Johnson's advisers was that the way to start an antipoverty initiative was with relatively small pilot projects, since no one knew from experience how best to solve the problem. Only a month or so after he had assumed the presidency, and with only a week or ten days before his first State of the Union speech, Johnson's advisers presented him the pilot projects approach at his ranch in Texas over the Christmas holidays. But Lyndon Johnson was not a man given to small, pilot projects; he wanted something big. Looking at the federal budget, Johnson found $500 million to spend on poverty and challenged his advisers to figure out how to use it.

When Johnson biographer Robert Caro asked presidential adviser Ted Sorensen about the origin of the phrase "war on poverty," Sorensen said it did not sound like something John Kennedy would have said, though it turns out that Kennedy had used it in a little-noted campaign speech in 1960.[1] Though no one seems to recall how the expression came into the discussion of LBJ's poverty initiatives, everyone agrees that Johnson himself readily embraced it. His adviser Elizabeth Wickenden recalled, "The whole idea of declaring a big war on poverty and ending it for all time, all the rhetoric of it, appealed to him very much."[2] Caro himself told NPR that Johnson "loved that phrase and it was part of his hatred of poverty," explaining that the causes of poverty were, to Johnson, "real-life foes and Johnson knew what to do with enemies: You destroyed them. So he loved the word 'war.' "[3]

What, then, do presidents gain by such a declaration of war? Part of its rhetorical value is the call to the nation to marshal its resources and move with speed and determination in a particular direction. Moreover, it built a kind of moral force behind anti-poverty programs that made it difficult for future presidents to cancel them later.[4] Indeed, in his recent book on Richard Nixon, adviser Pat Buchanan observed that Nixon decided not to challenge the war on poverty or other Great Society programs, leaving them largely in place.[5] Buchanan argues that this also fits a conservative pattern of not rolling back programs like the New Deal or the Great Society but, instead, accepting them as the new status quo.[6]

The legacy of the war on poverty, however, is mixed at best. President Ronald Reagan, in his January 25, 1988, State of the Union address, said, "Some years ago, the federal government declared war on poverty, and poverty won." Former President Eisenhower was less humorous but no less cynical about it, dismissing "catchily labeled panaceas—like 'war on poverty'— which usually turn out to be new channels by which even more power is siphoned into the federal government."[7] The conventional wisdom is that the war on poverty was not a success, and that poverty is as entrenched today as it was in 1964, perhaps even more so. As a report published in 2012 pointed out, however, more than $22 trillion has been spent on poverty programs since the war was declared. Perhaps that was the point: win or lose, a new bar had been set on antipoverty spending that is still actively pursued today.[8]

What we learn from the war on poverty is that a domestic policy war is rarely won. Indeed, we should not be surprised that a war on poverty, cooked up in short order as a matter of budgeting and presidential speechwriting, lacked serious attention to the policies the war would pursue. Even today, it would be difficult to find a clear and compelling philosophy behind the nation's antipoverty efforts. But the war did set a new moral imperative while establishing and funding a new set of programs that, on the one hand, have not succeeded but, on the other hand, have not been eliminated. The war on poverty established a new paradigm for moving the country in a particular direction in ways that were more difficult to reverse than mere programs. Nevertheless, such wars were short on policy and dubious in outcome.

The War on Crime

In 1964, Republican candidate Barry Goldwater, for the first time in a presidential campaign, made crime in the streets a fundamental issue, calling for "law and order" in the face of riots in America's cities. Following his election, in March 1965 President Lyndon Johnson had coupled his war on poverty with a war on crime, sending Congress the Law Enforcement Assistance Act. This broad new legislation, passed in the fall of 1965, brought the federal government into local law enforcement for the first time, providing federal involvement "in local police operations, court systems and state prisons."[9] The Office of Law Enforcement Assistance was created within the US Department of Justice to fund the war through grants to local law enforcement units. The goal, Johnson said in an address to Congress on March 9, 1966, was to "not only slow, but stop—and ultimately reverse—the rate of crime increase." The war accelerated with the passage of the Omnibus Safe Streets and Crime Control Act of 1968, giving block grants to states and broad powers to local law enforcement, including the controversial right to eavesdrop electronically.

Unlike Vietnam, this was not just Johnson's war. In his January 22, 1970, State of the Union message, President Richard Nixon commented on domestic wars more broadly and the war on crime specifically:

> We have heard a great deal of overblown rhetoric during the sixties in which the word "war" has perhaps too often been used—the war on poverty, the war on disease, the war on hunger. But if there is one area where the word "war" is appropriate it is in the fight against crime. We must declare and win the war against the criminal elements which increasingly threaten our cities, our homes, and our lives.

Nixon went on to acknowledge the primacy of local law enforcement, but concluded, "The federal government should play a greater role," proposing a doubling of federal spending in the area.

Although the war on crime continued during both Republican and Democratic administrations, the parties' underlying philosophies differed. For Democrats the war was primarily a question of social policy, improving the educational and economic outlooks for those who were turning to a life of crime.

For Republicans the war was basically about deterring crime and punishing the criminals, an approach advocated by criminologist James Q. Wilson in his important 1975 book *Thinking About Crime*. The war as carried out in the 1960s and 1970s was largely viewed as a failure. However, President Reagan relaunched the war in the 1980s, putting states on the front line to do most of the fighting, with federal assistance in sentencing and penalties provided by the Comprehensive Crime Control Act of 1984.[10]

The war on crime took on the character of an actual war as local law enforcement agencies purchased military equipment that had been used in Vietnam as part of their arsenal against rioting. Nevertheless, the national crime rate climbed, as did the percentage of the US population held in jails and prisons. The arming of local police for war in the streets was accelerated by the war on drugs and the war on terror. Today local police are frequently armed with helicopters, tanks, and other military-grade hardware fighting crime in the streets.

Now, more than fifty years following the declaration of the war on crime, one might ask about its consequences. In broad terms, crime continued to increase from the declaration of war for another twenty-five years, but finally, in 1990, it began to decline. Experts are not at all sure why, citing factors ranging from the improved economy and jobs picture to a larger number of police on the streets.[11] But obviously with the crime rate increasing into the 1990s, the war declared by Presidents Johnson and Nixon in the 1960s and 1970s had not been the solution.

Further, the war on crime has had other unintended policy consequences. In addition to federalizing what had previously been a local policy concern, the war on crime greatly militarized the approach to crime. The controversial police clashes and overreactions in places such as Ferguson, Missouri, in 2014 have raised the question whether the police have become too much like soldiers and too little like community law enforcement officers, turning drug dealers into "enemies" and communities into "war zones."[12] Critics have also begun to wonder whether we are jailing too many people because of the war on crime. As Yale law professor James Forman Jr. wrote, "[A]s the world's largest jailer we are increasingly desensitized to the harsh treatment of criminals. We have come to accept such excesses as casualties of war—whether on crime, drugs or terror."[13] Forman describes these problems as "the Wartime Overreaction Theory," noting that wars have casualties and innocent people are hurt.

Jonathan Simon, in his book *Governing Through Crime* (2009), advanced an argument very much aligned with our view, namely that a domestic war such as the war on crime had not only the effect but also the purpose of altering how America is governed. Simon argued that liberal elites were looking for issues that might allow for the expansion of the New Deal, perhaps using the welfare state or civil rights. But what they discovered was the platform of declaring domestic wars such as the war on crime. As he put it, "Americans have built a new civil and political structure around the problem of violent crime." Freedoms have been reduced and "new forms of power institutionalized and embraced" in the name of repressing violent crime.[14] The war metaphor in a field such as crime worked so well in expanding governance, Simon concluded, because of the "proximity to danger" (violent crime) "and the demands for power and knowledge that such proximity brings."[15]

From turning local law enforcement into a federal concern, to massive expenses on military equipment confronting citizens in the streets, to jailing large percentages of our population, one wonders whether any of this was truly contemplated when President Johnson first declared war on crime in 1965. A war has potentially huge consequences, for which the costs must be counted up front. Instead, politicians tend to react to a major crisis by feeling they must "do something," even if that turns out to be a lightly considered declaration of war. It seems doubtful that costs are fully counted and plans well developed when a domestic war, such as the war on crime, is declared.

The War on Drugs

Closely associated with the war on crime is the war on drugs, declared by President Richard Nixon in a press conference on June 17, 1971. "America's public enemy number one . . . is drug abuse," Nixon said, continuing that "[i]n order to defeat this enemy, it is necessary to wage a new, all-out offensive." Nixon added the specific term "war" in 1972, and by March 1973 he exhorted Congress that "this Administration has declared all-out global war on the drug menace." President Ford continued to use the term, which then became prolific under both Presidents Ronald Reagan and George H. W. Bush. As President Reagan, who appointed his own "drug czar," put it in 1986, "Drug abuse is a repudiation of everything America is."[16]

The notion of a war on drugs was problematic from the start. Who or what was the actual enemy? What tactics would be used? Were we attacking drug supplies (presumably from other countries) or demand among users in this country? Was this war primarily a law enforcement matter, or should it also concern health and treatment for users? What measurements of success would be used? When and how would we know that the war was being won? All these questions were debated but then largely buried in the broad rhetoric of war.

By now it is clear that the war on drugs was as much or more a political and rhetorical strategy undertaken by political leaders, as opposed to a carefully drawn set of policy measures. As Yale professor David Garland has written, "Motivated by the politically urgent need to 'do something' decisive about crime, in a context where the federal government mostly lacks jurisdiction (other areas of crime control being the prerogative of the states and local authorities) the war on drugs was the American state's attempt to 'just say no.'"[17] When President Bill Clinton was running for reelection and wanted to strengthen his "tough on crime" stance, he added an extra $1 billion to the war-on-drugs budget.[18]

One of the most notable outcomes of the war on drugs was a dramatic rise in the incarceration rate in the United States, as both dealers and those in possession of drugs faced mandatory jail sentences. Between 1980 and 2015, for example, the number of people in prison for drug offenses increased from some 40,000 to more than 400,000 and the average sentence more than tripled.[19] The majority of those sentenced were low-level offenders with no criminal record, and most were nonviolent offenders.[20] The war has been a huge contributor to the US status as having the largest prison population (more than 2.2 million people) in the world.

For some time, critics on both the left and the right have agreed that the war on drugs has not really solved the problem. Many liberals and conservatives alike have favored decriminalization of drugs, and in some cases outright legalization. Former secretary of state George Shultz, for example, wrote in his book *Issues on My Mind* that "the war on drugs that the United States has waged for decades has proved to be a losing battle," adding that "this paralleled the nation's experience with prohibition of alcohol."[21] Liberal senator Pat Leahy and conservative senator Rand Paul joined to sponsor a bill in 2017 to end mandatory sentences.

However, it is difficult to undertake a fundamental review of drug policy when we are at war. There is little opportunity to debate tough policy issues such as supply versus demand or treatment versus prevention during a war. And what happens when one domestic war is not coordinated with another war? For example, in a 2017 speech, Secretary of Housing and Urban

Development Ben Carson acknowledged, "The war on poverty sometimes conflicted with the war on drugs, which often dealt harshly with nonviolent offenders, taking men away from their families, and disproportionately affecting minority communities."[22] But at the same time, President Donald Trump and Attorney General Jeff Sessions appeared to be doubling down on the war on drugs, urging more federal prosecution and longer sentences, and leaving no real space for policy deliberation. Indeed the very idea of being at war is that the effort is continuous with few limitations or boundaries.[23] The rhetoric is not one of policy or solutions but rather one of continuous war.[24] Meanwhile, the drug problem escalates and the war carries on, with new enemies (opioids) and new strategies (a border wall).

Jimmy Carter's "Moral Equivalent of War" on Energy Consumption

On April 18, 1977, President Jimmy Carter delivered a prime-time televised address about "a problem that is unprecedented in our history," and with the exception of preventing war, "the greatest challenge that our country will face during our lifetime." The issue, as Carter described it in that speech, was to "balance our demand for energy with our rapidly shrinking resources." But the deeper challenge Carter confronted was motivating the American people, at least half of whom either did not believe there was an energy crisis or thought that it had been artificially created.[25]

Carter understood that the way presidents had come to motivate action, both by Congress and by the people, is by declaring a state of war on a domestic problem, in this case energy consumption. Indeed, he was quite explicit about this, acknowledging in his televised address that "[t]his difficult effort will be the 'moral equivalent of war,' except that we will be uniting our efforts to build and not to destroy." So it was to be a war but a constructive, not a destructive one, which is not entirely consistent with the meaning of the term. But this is how presidents since LBJ had led their most important domestic priorities, by borrowing the language of war.

As with other domestic war efforts, such as the war on poverty, Carter's moral equivalent of war was short on policy specifics. All he offered in the address were "ten fundamental principles" on which a national energy plan would be based. In this same time frame, Carter expanded federal oversight of all energy issues by establishing the US Department of Energy in August 1977. As if to underscore the need for war, the White House took the unusual step of releasing a CIA report predicting major price increases for oil "unless large-scale conservation measures cut demand sharply."[26] As Hedrick Smith wrote in the *New York Times* shortly after the speech, Carter "had chosen energy on which to test and build his Presidential leadership."[27] Once again, a president would call for sacrifice and new policies against the specter of war, and on that basis enhance his presidential power.

Carter's use of the term "moral equivalent of war" came from a speech delivered at Stanford University by psychologist and philosopher William James in 1906, later published as an essay in 1910 with that same title. In the essay, James argued for using the war metaphor as a way to lead the society toward greater national service. He felt that the discipline, sacrifice, and purposefulness of the war metaphor could help rally Americans toward peaceful purposes, something that political scientist Wilfred McClay correctly observed "has informed most Progressive efforts to build a comprehensively organized and morally purposeful nation."[28] And so now we have real wars; the war metaphor to advance domestic priorities; and, thanks to Jimmy Carter, the moral equivalent of war.

The War on Terror

Although domestic wars are the focus of concern, one cannot help but notice an overlap between military wars and those declared as a matter of domestic policy. For example, the first domestic wars, those on poverty and crime, were declared during the Vietnam War. And the war on terror, declared by President George W. Bush in response to the 9/11 attacks in New York City and on the Pentagon, has many parallels with the domestic wars still being fought.

The war on terror was initially a somewhat limited war focused on Al-Qaeda. But wars tend to grow, and now the Costs of War Project at Brown University's Watson Institute for International and Public Affairs identifies seventy-six countries, or 39 percent of the world, involved in that conflict.[29] During the war on terror, the number of terrorist groups has grown from 28 in 2002 to 61 today.[30] The war in Afghanistan, which is part of the war on terror, is now the longest war in American history, and it continues. Though experts will debate the question of cause and effect, like the wars on poverty, crime, and drugs, the war on terror is accompanied by more terror and more war.

As with domestic wars, identifying the enemy has been a challenge in the war on terror. The three presidents on whose watch this war has been fought have used various terms such as "terrorists," "violent extremists," or simply "the enemy" to lump together dozens of different groups around the world.[31] At first it was a "war on terror," but then it became a "war on terrorism," with the awkwardness of fighting means and tools of war rather than people. The congressional authorization for the war—the Authorization for Use of Military Force (AUMF)—in 2001 was to use force against the perpetrators of the 9/11 attacks, but it is still in effect and has been steadily expanded by presidents in the twenty-first century to include the Islamic State and others.

Finally, like domestic wars, the war on terror has been expensive and seemingly without end. Present estimates on the cost of the war run as high as $5.6 trillion, with no end in sight. Like the wars on poverty, crime, and drugs, we seem to be in a perpetual state of war, with little opportunity to review our policies and our purposes, only the tactics. Like the wars on crime and drugs, the war footing has placed the military out front in our foreign policy, even as we reduce the number and role of diplomats in the State Department.

Emergencies May Come and Go, but Emergency Powers Remain

Most Americans would not be aware that they are living in a state of national emergency—in recent years, twenty-eight to thirty of them at a time. Although slightly different in character from the domestic wars presidents have launched against poverty, crime, and the like, these national emergencies declared by presidents nevertheless have a significant effect and, added together, reinforce the constant sense of living in wars and emergencies. The oldest national emergency still operative was declared by President Jimmy Carter during the 1979 Iran hostage crisis, which means we are living in our thirty-ninth consecutive year of national emergency.

Although the Constitution does not explicitly give the president power to declare national emergencies, this has long been part of our practice. In the 1970s, when Congress reexamined executive power in the wake of Watergate and the Vietnam War, concern arose about the number and scope of presidentially declared national emergencies. At that time, there were four national emergencies still in effect, the oldest from the New Deal era: Franklin Roosevelt's national bank holiday declaration. Congress passed, and President Gerald Ford signed in 1976, the National Emergencies Act (NEA), to limit and control presidential declarations of national emergency.

Unfortunately, the NEA did not accomplish its goal, since as many as twenty-eight national emergencies are now in effect, with all the rights, privileges, and duties thereto appertaining. These emergencies cover everything from vessels near Cuba, democratic processes in Zimbabwe, and exporting goods to Syria and Liberia, to cyber warfare, export control regulations, and narcotics trafficking. Although earlier presidents employed these powers more modestly, beginning with President Bill Clinton, who enacted seventeen national emergencies, the use of these powers has grown. As Justice Robert Jackson predicted in the famous *Youngstown Sheet & Tube Co. v. Sawyer* decision in 1952 concerning President Truman's emergency declaration about steel, "[The Founders] knew what emergencies were, knew the pressures they engender for authoritative action, knew, too, how they afford a ready pretext for usurpation. We may also suspect that they suspected that emergency powers would tend to kindle emergencies."

The ability to make a unilateral declaration of a national emergency represents a significant expansion of presidential power. As Professor Kim Lane Scheppele of Princeton University has said, "What the National Emergencies Act does is like a toggle switch, and when the president flips it, he gets new powers. It's like a magic wand, and there are very few constraints about how he turns it on."[32] And these national emergencies span a broad range of powers. An excellent article by Patrick A. Thronson on national emergencies notes that "[e]ach emergency activates powers in over 160 provisions of statutory law, dozens of presidential orders, and numerous other federal regulations."[33]

A major reason these national emergencies persist for decades is that Congress has fallen down on the job assigned to it by

the National Emergencies Act. Under the law, Congress is supposed to vote every six months on whether a national emergency
should continue, but this is not done. As a result, one more important matter that is supposed to be a shared responsibility between Congress and the president has become the purview of
the president only. As we have seen elsewhere, executive power
does not grow only because of an aggressive president, but also
because of a passive and disinterested Congress. Clearly Congress needs to step up to the plate and meets its responsibilities in
this area. When there are nearly thirty states of emergency, essentially decided only by the president, you are a long way from
the kind of governance the Constitution, and even the National
Emergencies Act, contemplated.

The Effects of Domestic Wars

Declaring "war" on a domestic problem would seem to be primarily metaphorical and rhetorical. But since the bully pulpit
has long been recognized as a powerful tool of the presidency,
such rhetorical and metaphorical value should not be min-
imized. Declaring a domestic war has been within the president's sole power, only requiring Congress to follow along later
with spending to support it. Such a declaration calls forth a
government-wide priority and effort, spanning all agencies and
offices. Though other policies may come and go, wars on domestic problems seemingly have no end, as decades later we continue
to fight wars on poverty, crime, drugs, and the like. In few other

ways can a president put such a powerful long-term stake in the ground of domestic policy.

Further, declaring war on a domestic problem turns out to be a way for the federal government to extend its power into matters previously thought to be the province of state or local governments. Especially in the case of crime, and its close cousins drugs and terrorism, the primary responsibility has long belonged to local law enforcement. But by declaring a federal war on crime, Washington, DC, first began to provide funding and equipment to local law enforcement, changing the character of the war, and then moved into more direct control of the matter, changing standards of prosecution, sentencing, and so forth. The whole debate of federal versus state control was obviated by declaring war on a major national problem and calling forth all players, especially those from Washington, to battle.

The notion that we were a nation at war has had a powerful effect on the policy landscape. The whole approach to welfare became a federal issue with the war on poverty. Crime became a literal war, with military weapons brought from the federal government onto the local battlefield. Our prison population grew dramatically with active prosecution and minimum sentencing laws, with a profound impact on our inner cities. Constitutional protections of civil rights and free speech were challenged by our federal war on terror, or as it was later called, terrorism. None of these major policy shifts had been matters of significant debate—rather they were fallouts of presidents declaring and waging domestic war.

For our purposes, a crucial outcome is a change not just in policy but also in process. Deliberation, which the Founders had understood to be a fundamental approach of government leading to compromise or stalemate, was replaced in all these areas by war and action, which lead to victory or defeat. Lyndon Johnson wanted action on poverty and, having found some federal money to invest, told his executive branch advisers to find a way to spend it. Underlying the war on drugs was the key policy dilemma of treatment versus law enforcement. But if you're the federal government, what you have is money and equipment and control of federal laws. So over time the war on drugs became much less about treatment and prevention and much more about law enforcement, prosecution, and imprisonment. The nuances and balances of policy are nearly impossible to deliberate over when you are at war. And so the domestic war became a new tool of "action, and action now" for modern presidents.

Presidents Leveraging War Powers Abroad into Domestic Powers at Home

In addition to creating wars over domestic priorities, modern wartime presidents have been able to increase their powers at home by leveraging their commander-in-chief role from international conflicts. Beginning with Lyndon Johnson and Richard Nixon from the Vietnam War and extending through George W. Bush, Barack Obama, and Donald Trump in the war on terror, the overall powers of the executive have grown during war. Perhaps this is purposeful, based on cause and effect, or perhaps it is merely a natural spillover from one arena to the other, but nevertheless this effect has added to the president's domestic power and to the sense of war at home. Indeed, some of the presidents thought of as the most powerful in the modern era, especially Johnson and Nixon, were wartime presidents.

The Great Society Revolution

Lyndon Johnson became a wartime president—in fact, the war in Vietnam was often referred to as "Johnson's war." As a wartime president, Johnson sought to expand the president's power to engage in and direct the war, while limiting the involvement of Congress. As journalist Tom Wicker wrote, "The Tonkin Gulf resolution he maneuvered through Congress left him and for a while Nixon virtually a free hand in Indochina; and in waging one of the largest wars in American history without Congressional declaration, Johnson notably expanded the already extensive 'war powers' of the presidency."[34] The president unilaterally decided war strategy, increased troop levels regularly, and even selected bombing targets. In fact, Congress passed the War Powers Act of 1973 largely in response to Johnson's (and Nixon's) overreach.

Johnson seemed comfortable carrying his war rhetoric and the war metaphor over into his domestic policies. His bold Great Society vision would, he said at the University of Michigan on May 22, 1964, be a "battle" to build. And his first major project was a "war on poverty," declared in his first State of the Union message, on January 8, 1964. It would not be enough to have antipoverty "programs" or "policies" but rather we would declare war on this domestic enemy. As noted earlier, this domestic war was soon joined by a "war on crime," bringing the federal war metaphor full bore into America's cities. These domestic wars have even outlasted the lengthy war in Vietnam, and have built the model that has been followed by other presidents who declared war on domestic problems.

We can readily find a connection between Johnson's expanded powers as a war president abroad and his development of enhanced presidential powers at home. Johnson's biographer Robert Caro has described him as "the man who used political power better than any president from the second half of the 20th century."[35] Johnson himself admitted, "I do understand power, whatever else may be said about me. I know where to look for it, and how to use it."[36] Although he used a goodly number of executive orders, for example, during his five-year presidency, he also built out the modern presidency by adding two new cabinet departments: Housing and Urban Development in 1965 and Transportation in 1966.

But it was Johnson's leadership of Congress where his power was most clearly manifest. Having been the powerful Senate majority leader himself, Johnson knew and understood the levers of legislative power. He recognized, for example, the importance of counting votes—as Robert Caro has said, the businessman's equivalent of following the balance sheet.[37] He knew the intricacies of legislative debates and voting and how to lobby members of Congress.[38] He gave legislators "The Treatment," a close-up, personal, and even physically intimidating session with the larger-than-life president. In his aptly titled book for our theme of war and emergency, *The Fierce Urgency of Now*, Julian E. Zelizer concludes that Johnson was "truly determined to expand the role of the federal government in domestic life far beyond what his hero Franklin Roosevelt had accomplished."[39] In many ways, Johnson epitomized the war and emergency approach to governance, growing the modern presidency ever further in power.

Nixon and the Imperial Presidency

Although it is true that presidential power and governing by wars and emergencies did not grow in a straight line in the modern era, it would be a mistake to say, as some might have predicted, that it grew only during Democratic presidencies and shrank during Republican administrations. Indeed, if Lyndon Johnson was thought of as the most effective president in wielding presidential power since Franklin Roosevelt, his Republican successor, Richard Nixon, was characterized as having created "an imperial presidency."[40]

Nixon inherited and continued to wage a large-scale war in Vietnam and beyond, and he maintained strong presidential authority over the war. When Congress passed the War Powers Act of 1973, limiting a president's authority to declare war without Congress, Nixon vetoed it, though Congress overrode his veto. But like Johnson, Nixon also undertook war and emergency powers in his domestic agenda and continued building out a strong modern presidency. In fact, compared with a conservative president such as Ronald Reagan, Nixon led the federal government into proactive policies about the environment and the economy, so that one might argue that he was not a truly conservative president.

Perhaps most important for our purposes is that Nixon carried on Johnson's domestic wars on poverty and, especially, crime. Noting Johnson's domestic wars, Nixon observed, "If there is one area where the 'war' is appropriate it is in the fight against crime."[41] Notably Nixon also launched a new domestic war on drugs, which continues to grow in both scope and controversy today. When he signed a bill devoting significant additional resources to the battle against cancer, it was referred to, although not by Nixon himself, as a war on cancer.[42] So domestic policy wars, both declared and undeclared, grew significantly under Nixon's leadership.

Nixon was also active in the issuance of executive orders, signing 346 in his five-plus years as president. His creation of the Environmental Protection Agency in 1970 launched one of those most proactive and highly regulatory efforts of the federal government. Nixon surprised the nation by unilaterally declaring wage and price controls in the summer of 1971, a bold exercise of executive leadership that was constitutionally suspect. Even though the economy was not in bad shape by historic measures, Nixon found a sufficient basis for emergency presidential action. More broadly, Nixon shifted power from cabinet offices to the

Executive Office of the President, where his personal aides, John Ehrlichman and H. R. Haldeman, presided over groups such as the Domestic Policy Council and increasingly ran the government and its policies from the White House.

However, Nixon's biggest domestic war was about Watergate, battling Congress and the courts over executive power before finally resigning the presidency. The whole range of presidential action was quite stunning—from taking over operation of the 1972 campaign from the Republican National Committee to creating "the plumbers" who broke into Democratic National Committee headquarters. Nixon drafted a clear sign of war, an "enemies list," and expanded notions of executive privilege to prevent his closest aides from testifying before Congress. He created a constitutional crisis—firing an independent prosecutor, accepting resignations of attorneys general, and battling in federal courts—before he finally resigned, closing at least this chapter of the imperial presidency.

George W. Bush, Barack Obama, and Donald Trump: A War on Terror, Both Abroad and at Home

Although George W. Bush emphasized his ability, as governor of Texas, to work across the aisle with both parties, and he preached "compassionate conservatism" to try to heal policy divides, he became essentially a war president following the attacks of 9/11. A war president often grows executive power not only for the conflict abroad, but also at home, and such was the case with Bush. Because the war on terror he launched has continued, and is a war with domestic dimensions, executive power both at home and abroad has continued to grow.

The war declared by President George W. Bush was unlike any other. Following the 9/11 attacks on the World Trade Center in New York and the Pentagon, the president first declared a "war on terror," later adjusting the language to a "war on terrorism." By not specifying a particular nation as the enemy, the war took on global proportions. Because the first attack of the war was at home, and it was believed that the homeland continued to be a target, the war had huge domestic implications. As noted earlier, the war continues nearly two decades later, with no end in sight. As a consequence, the possibilities for the growth of executive power in this war have been unusually great.

The president did seek congressional approval for the war, with the Authorization for Use of Military Force (AUMF) "seeking, perhaps the broadest grant of war power by Congress since World War II," according to presidential legal adviser John Yoo.[43] But the president's war powers did not stop there. The president authorized surveillance of the homeland through unprecedented domestic wiretapping and eavesdropping as well as review of email. Bush ordered that the Geneva Conventions did not apply, starting America down the road toward the use of torture. The president began issuing signing statements, noting his objections to portions of laws passed by Congress, even though he signed the bills. As his legal defender John Yoo acknowledged, "President Bush reached for a broad vision of executive power."[44]

Experts generally agree that President George W. Bush significantly increased executive power, and not just over the conduct of a war abroad. Political scientist James Pfiffner argues that presidential power ratchets up over time, rather than swinging back and forth like a pendulum, and that Bush "created precedents of constitutional claims" that made the presidency "more powerful," enabling future presidents to say "Bush did it."[45] Gene Healy, vice president at the Cato Institute, believes that the Bush administration was "articulating as broad as any theory of presidential power offered by any administration in history."[46]

Presidential historian Arthur Schlesinger has argued that a president's power increases during wartime but recedes in peacetime.[47] Moreover, those powers are not limited to war, but flow over into domestic policy: "If the President were conceded these life-and-death decisions abroad," Schlesinger asks, "how could he be restrained from gathering unto himself the less fateful powers of the national policy?"[48] In the "interminable and pervasive 'war against terror'" Schlesinger sees "a threat to the nation's system of governance."[49] Indeed, President Bush's lawyer saw a similar rise in executive power for a related reason: "the United States . . . became an empire."[50] If the United States remains in a nearly permanent war on terror, the rise of executive power over that of Congress will be a continuing issue.

Even though presidential candidate Barack Obama was critical of Bush's exercise of presidential power and conduct of the war on terror, as president he ultimately followed the same path Bush had charted. Then-senator Obama criticized the war on terror in a speech on October 2, 2002, referring to it as a "dumb war" and a "rash war . . . based not on reason but on passion, not on principle but on politics." He said, "Saddam [Hussein] poses no imminent and direct threat to the United States or his neighbors." In a presidential debate on November 15, 2007, he criticized President Bush's legal overreach in the conduct of the war, saying that he would "lead by shutting down Guantánamo and restoring habeas corpus in this country." As president, Obama avoided the term "war on terror" and sought not to have his administration defined by the war, as Bush's had been.

Over time, however, President Obama ended up retaining most of the policies and even increasing some of the powers President Bush had established through the war on terror. For example, on his second day in office Obama issued an executive order to close the Guantánamo Bay detention camp as soon as practicable and no later than one year from the date of the order, but the facility remains open even today in the Trump administration. Similarly, he pledged to discontinue use of the Authorization to Use Military Force (AUMF), but instead its application grew and it, too, remains in effect. The Obama administration ended up surpassing that of President Bush in the use of drones and special forces in the war, in National Security Agency surveillance of civilians, and in prosecuting those who leaked information to reporters.[51]

James Madison observed that "war is the true nurse of executive aggrandizement," and that proved to be true in the Obama experience. Intending as a candidate to phase down the war and reduce the exercise of executive powers, as president he did just the opposite. Michael Hayden, director of the CIA under

Bush, agreed that there was a "continuity" between the Bush and Obama approaches to the war and to the exercise of war powers.[52] Any differences between Bush and Obama on the war turned out to be more rhetorical than real; meanwhile, the national security apparatus of war became permanent. The first year of the Trump administration brought no real change to the war on terror or executive power. The AUMF is still in effect, Guantánamo is still open, and bombing has increased as both the war and the president's war powers continue to grow.[53]

We should note that William G. Howell, a political scientist at the University of Chicago, has questioned whether a president's war powers actually do flow over into increased domestic powers in a way that is demonstrable. In an article in the *Annual Review of Political Science* in 2011,[54] Howell reviewed the "largely consensual view that wars naturally and reflexively augment presidential power," a case advanced by Edward Corwin, Clinton Rossiter, and Arthur Schlesinger. Unable to find quantifiable evidence that Congress and the judiciary act differently toward a president in war or peace, Howell questioned whether there is sufficient "unambiguous evidence" to support the conventional wisdom about the growth of presidential power during war.

While an important inquiry, one wonders whether Howell is seeking the right kind of evidence to answer his question. The war as metaphor, with its attendant power and influence, is different from an empirical approach and thus the standard of what is and what is not reliable evidence would be different. Indeed, ambiguity is part of political life and of the metaphorical approach. Further, our argument is that, beginning with

Franklin Roosevelt and his call to "action, and action now," the entire relationship between Congress and the president began to shift in both wartime and peacetime. Congress began to defer to the president, who in turn became the initiator and leader, even constructing domestic wars and emergencies to increase his ability to act.

Hyperpartisanship and Gridlock Grow Presidential Power and Increase Domestic Warfare

We live in a time of hyperpartisanship and government gridlock, with the war metaphor increasingly ruling the day. Supreme Court nominations result in full-scale battles, with debates over whether to deploy "the nuclear option." On seemingly every issue, battle lines are drawn and there is little or no deliberation. The most important legislation of the Obama years, the Affordable Care Act, was passed on a party-line vote, with no Republicans voting in favor, while the most important legislation of the Trump era thus far, tax reform, was passed on a straight party-line vote with no Democrats in favor. Bills are held in secret until fifty-one votes are available in the Senate, and then they are hurried onto the floor with little debate and few amendments.

This warlike atmosphere in domestic politics can be traced, in part, to the 2004 presidential election. Historically modern presidential campaigns had been a race to the center, with a bloc of

Republican voters on the right and another bloc of Democrats on the left, and candidates seeking to reach the voters in the middle to win. Richard Nixon famously said he had to run to the right to win the Republican nomination and then to the center to win the election. But George W. Bush's campaign adviser Karl Rove changed all that by designing a different way to win the presidency: turning out your base. By 2004, the number of independents in the center had dropped and it became possible to win by turning out your base. Appealing to your base can result in an ugly campaign, focusing on narrow issues that appeal to segments of voters and portraying your opponent as an awful enemy.

With Karl Rove in the White House as the director of political affairs, this same approach was used in governing. Rove's idea was to build a new long-term Republican majority by playing to its base in government policy.[55] Rather than pursuing bipartisan ideas such as No Child Left Behind in the first term, Rove saw an opportunity post-9/11 to build a conservative national security base, and began developing a set of conservative policy ideas to feed it, including faith-based initiatives, privatizing Social Security, and the like. Part of the strategy involved engaging the president in a continuous campaign of war, stirring up the base more than actually governing.[56]

Barack Obama famously ran against this sort of base-oriented view of politics and governing. In his campaign of 2008, he called for a politics of "hope and change." Presenting himself as a "post-partisan" politician, Obama said he would turn the page on the "ugly partisanship" in Washington. As it turned out, however, partisanship grew during his presidency, with blue states becoming bluer and red states redder.[57] The president proposed a bold agenda and Republicans in Congress resisted, leading to the passage of his signature legislation, the Affordable Care Act, on a straight party-line vote of Democrats. Obama and Congress continued to frustrate one another until, early in his second term, the president said he had "a pen and a phone" and would seek to take unilateral action through executive orders and vetoes if necessary to get things done. The president proceeded to use executive orders, not to execute the law, but to make new law in areas such as immigration reform and gun control, and he unilaterally altered the Obamacare law several times.[58] This increased use of executive power in the face of gridlock exacerbated the warlike atmosphere in Washington.

Donald Trump continued the heavy use of executive power by seeking to undo several of Obama's executive orders early in his administration. Indeed, one of the problems of executive orders is that they can be easily overturned so that a president, like Obama, who carried out much of his agenda in this way can find his legacy quickly undone by the next president.[59] A government in gridlock then becomes a battlefield for dueling executive orders and party-line votes, all subject to reversal by a subsequent administration or Congress. A nation already in domestic war and national emergencies now finds itself subject to further unproductive battles in Washington and greater use of unilateral executive powers.

NOTES

1. Robert A. Caro, *The Years of Lyndon Johnson: The Passage of Power* (New York: Vintage Books, 2012), 544–45.

2. Ibid., 545.

3. NPR, "For LBJ, the War on Poverty Was Personal," January 8, 2014, www.npr.org/2014/01/08/260572/for-lbj-the-war-on-poverty-was-personal.

4. Ibid.

5. Patrick J. Buchanan, *Nixon's White House Wars* (New York: Crown Forum, 2017), 26.

6. Ibid., 45.

7. *Los Angeles Times*, "Hits Centralized Rule: Eisenhower Explains Why He's Republican," April 5, 1964.

8. We doubt the 2018 report by the President's Council of Economic Advisers that the war on poverty is "largely over." See David Davenport, "Foolhardy Presidents Keep Declaring 'War' on Problems They Can't Solve," *Washington Examiner,* July 24, 2018, https://www.washingtonexaminer.com/opinion/foolhardy-presidents-keep-declaring-war-on-problems-they-cant-solve.

9. Elizabeth Hinton, "Why We Should Reconsider the War on Crime," *Time,* March 20, 2015.

10. John J. DiIulio, Jr., "A Limited War on Crime That We Can Win: Two Lost Wars Later," *The Brookings Review* 10, no. 4 (Fall 1992): 8.

11. See, e.g., Matt Ford, "What Caused the Great Crime Decline in the U.S.?," *The Atlantic,* April 15, 2016.

12. See, e.g., Elizabeth Price Foley, "The 'War' Against Crime: Ferguson, Police Militarization and the Third Amendment," *Tennessee Law Review* 82 (2015): 583–86.

13. James Forman, Jr., "Exporting Harshness: How the War on Crime Helped Make the War on Terror Possible," *NYU Review of Law and Social Change* 33 (2009): 333.

14. Jonathan Simon, *Governing Through Crime* (New York: Oxford University Press, 2007), 3–4.

15. Ibid., 260.

16. Matthew R. Pembleton, "We've Spent a Century Fighting the War on Drugs. It Helped Create an Opioid Crisis," *Washington Post,* August 31, 2017.

17. David Garland, *The Culture of Control* (Chicago: University of Chicago Press, 2001), 132.

18. Keesha M. Middlemass, "Chapter Six: War as Metaphor," in *The War on Poverty,* ed. Kyle Farmbry (Boulder, CO: Lexington Books, 2014), 93.

19. Joel Gunter, "Officers Rue the Return of US 'War on Drugs,'" *BBC News,* April 18, 2017, http://www.bbc.com/news/world-us-canada-39623671, accessed December 19, 2017.

20. Ibid.

21. George P. Shultz, *Issues on My Mind* (Stanford, CA: Hoover Institution Press, 2013), 53, 56.

22. Brian Doherty, "Ben Carson Admits War on Drugs Conflicts with War on Poverty," http://reason.com/blog/2017/12/19/ben-carson-admits-war-on-drugs-conflicts, accessed December 19, 2017.

23. See Middlemass, *The War on Poverty*, 86.

24. See Susan Stuart, "War as Metaphor and the Rule of Law in Crisis: The Lessons We Should Have Learned from the War on Drugs," *Southern Illinois University Law Journal* 36, no. 1 (2011): 1-2.

25. Charles Mohr, "Carter Asks Strict Fuel Saving: Urges 'Moral Equivalent of War' to Bar a 'National Catastrophe,'" *New York Times*, April 19, 1977.

26. Ibid.

27. Hedrick Smith, "A Test of Leadership," *New York Times*, April 21, 1977, 39.

28. Wilfred M. McClay, "The Moral Equivalent of War?," *National Affairs* (Fall 2010).

29. See http://watson.brown.edu/costsofwar/. See also, Tom Engelhardt, "A New Map Shows the Alarming Spread of the U.S. War on Terror," *The Nation*, January 4, 2018, https://www.thenation.com/article/a-new-map-shows-the-alarming-spread-of-the-us-war-on-terror/, accessed January 18, 2018.

30. Micah Zenko, "Bush and Obama Fought a Failed 'War on Terror.' It's Trump's Turn," *New York Times*, August 25, 2017.

31. Ibid.

32. Gregory Korte, "America's Perpetual State of Emergency," *USA Today*, October 22, 2014.

33. Patrick A. Thronson, "Toward Comprehensive Reform of America's Emergency Law Regime," *University of Michigan Journal of Law Reform* 46, no. 2 (2013): 753.

34. Tom Wicker, *One of Us: Richard Nixon and the American Dream* (New York: Random House, 1971), 677.

35. Interview with Robert Caro, *PBS Newshour*, May 10, 2012, http://www.pbs.org/newshour/politics/author-caro-lbj-used-full-potential-of-presidential-power, accessed January 25, 2018.

36. Diane Coutu, "Lessons in Power: Lyndon Johnson Revealed," *Harvard Business Review*, April 2006.

37. Ibid.

38. Julian E. Zelizer, *The Fierce Urgency of Now* (New York: Penguin Books, 2015).

39. Ibid., 2.

40. Arthur M. Schlesinger, Jr., *The Imperial Presidency* (New York: Houghton Mifflin, 1973).

41. Stephanie Condon, "Is It Time to End the War on Crime?," CBSNews.com, April 3, 2015, accessed December 22, 2017.

42. Sabin Russell, "Nixon's War on Cancer: Why It Mattered," September 21, 2016, https://www.fredhutch.org/en/news/center-news/2016/09/nixons-war-on-cancer-and-why-it-mattered.html, accessed January 26, 2018.

43. John Yoo, *Crisis and Command* (New York: Kaplan Publishing, 2009), 411.

44. Ibid., 417.

45. Warren Richey, "Bush Pushed the Limits of Presidential Power," *Christian Science Monitor*, January 14, 2009.

46. Ibid.

47. Arthur Schlesinger, *The Imperial Presidency*.

48. Ibid., ix.

49. William G. Howell, "Presidential Power in War," *Annual Review of Political Science* (2011): 93.

50. Yoo, *Crisis and Command*, 404.

51. Linda Feldmann, "Is Barack Obama an Imperial President?," *Christian Science Monitor*, January 26, 2014.

52. David Kravets, "Former CIA Chief: Obama's War on Terror Same as Bush's, but with More Killing," *Wired*, September 2012. See also, Peter Baker, "Obama's War on Terror," *New York Times*, January 4, 2010.

53. Micah Zenko, "Bush and Obama Fought a Failed 'War on Terror.' It's Trump's Turn," *New York Times*, August 25, 2017.

54. William G. Howell, "Presidential Power in War," *Annual Review of Political Science* 14, no. 1 (2011): 89–105.

55. See Julian E. Zelizer, "Dissecting 'Bush's Brain," *Politico*, August 13, 2007, https://www.politico.com/story/2007/08/dissecting-bushs-brain-005367, accessed March 16, 2018.

56. Lewis Gould, "Stop the Campaigning," *Washington Post*, October 30, 2005.

57. Matt Viser, "Obama's Vision of Unity Led Only to a Wider Gap," *Boston Globe*, October 14, 2013.

58. David Davenport, "Obama's Executive Power Pen Is Already Worn Out," Forbes.com, February 24, 2014, https://www.forbes.com/sites/daviddavenport/2014/02/24/obamas-executive-power-pen-is-already-worn-out/#379ac04d77e6, accessed March 17, 2018.

59. David Davenport, "How Trump Managed to Undo Obama's Legacy in One Week," Forbes.com, January 27, 2017, https://www.forbes.com/sites/daviddavenport/2017/01/27/how-trump-managed-to-undo-obamas-legacy-in-one-week/#50f0253a1c4f, accessed March 17, 2018.

4 What Public Policy Was Supposed to Be

DELIBERATION AT THE FOUNDING

Now we go back to come back. We go back into history, specifically to the founding era of the American republic, to gain a better understanding of how our system of government was designed to work, in order to come back and see whether those principles still apply to public policy today. Has a system intended to function in a particular way now been diverted to new methods that quite simply do not work? Can we learn something from the Founders that would still work today?

The Founders faced the same tensions in constructing a "democratic republic" that we confront governing and living in one today. On the one hand, they were committed to liberty, which was the grand promise of the Declaration of Independence. Americans were to be free to pursue happiness, with as few limitations, especially from their government, as possible. On the other hand, the new nation was also committed to equality, again a pillar of the Declaration that "all men are created equal." But then, as now, these two pillars exist in tension, requiring the protection of a republican form of government and constant deliberation.

The accusation frequently made against the Founders today is that they created republican structures to thwart the democratic voice of the people. But structures such as separations of power, checks and balances, and the like actually exist to protect against hasty action and to promote deliberation. The Founders feared a pure, unfiltered democracy in which this or that faction might run the country aground in one or another rash direction. Instead, they sought a full deliberative process that would both achieve the goals of the people and ensure a careful, thoughtful decision-making process.

We do not advocate mimicking what the Founders said and did. One of their important teachings is that each generation must learn for itself the difficult art of self-government. The Founders warned against "a blind veneration for antiquity" (*Federalist* No. 14), and Thomas Jefferson famously wrote, "the earth . . . belongs to the living." Thus, we counsel a careful understanding and enlightened veneration of the Founders in seeking to understand the purposes and practices of deliberation.

The Founders Built a Government of, by, and for Deliberation

The Founders of the American republic practiced what they preached. Their purpose was to establish a government of deliberation and, in so doing, they demonstrated deliberation both indoors, in the halls of formal deliberation, and out of doors, in speeches and writings. In this way they not only designed structures of government that would enhance deliberation, but they also gave a public exhibition of how it should be done. They drafted, debated, amended, persuaded, and compromised their way to a new form of government.

And what was the purpose of all this deliberation? As the Founders themselves said in *The Federalist*, it was to find the cool, deliberate sense of the community over time as the North Star toward which the republic should move. Not the heated passions of the moment, surely, but the more settled and fully developed views of the people were the object. James Madison described it most clearly in *Federalist* No. 63 when, in defending the Senate as a protection against "temporary errors and delusions" of the people, said, "[T]he cool and deliberate sense of the community ought in all government ultimately prevail." Alexander Hamilton confirmed this in *Federalist* No. 71 and turned it into what he called "the republican principle," namely that "the deliberate sense of the community should govern the conduct of those to whom they entrust the management of their affairs."

And how else to find true north—the cool and deliberate sense of the community—than by employing the navigational tools of deliberation? The people should deliberate, but equally important, so should their elected representatives. Especially in founding the republic, leaders should see "the necessity of sacrificing private opinions and partial interests to the public good" (*Federalist* No. 37). At all times that would require withstanding the temporary inclinations of the people to look out for their longer-term interests, "in order to give them time and opportunity for more cool and sedate reflection" (*Federalist* No. 71).

"We, the people" should be heard in a democracy, but our views should be refined through the constitutional processes of checks and balances and separations of power. The Founders' republic would not be a pure Athenian democracy with everyone meeting in a public square to make policy decisions, but rather a representative democracy resting on the practice of deliberation. The three branches of government would check and balance one another and, in the case of the most powerful branch, the legislature, two different houses with varying electoral terms and rules would limit each other. Ambition would counteract ambition in the enlarged republic of the United States. All of this constitutional process was carefully laid out to protect and move forward with the cool, deliberate sense of the community. If, in the view of the Founders, pure democracy was a problem, then deliberation was the solution: deliberation made democracy safe for the world.

This is a far cry from collecting fifty-one party-line votes in the Senate to enact policy, as is frequently done today. No longer do we even bring a matter to the floor of the US Senate, for example, unless we're certain our side has the votes to prevail. The point is no longer to deliberate, but to win. We limit debate and the opportunity for amendments. The leadership sometimes even holds bills in secret until they are fully drafted and ready to spring on Congress, as if by surprise. The quest is not to find the cool, deliberate sense of the people, but to enact legislation, often on party-line votes, that will please one side or the other. Even "bipartisanship" and "compromise" have become dirty words. For the Founders, making policy was about something else entirely: it was about deliberation.

Deliberation Indoors: The Constitutional Convention and the Ratifying Conventions

The first sentence of the first paragraph of the first essay in *The Federalist* underscores the opportunity and obligation that was set before the founding generation: "You are called upon to deliberate on a new Constitution for the United States of America." And deliberate they did. Some two thousand elected officials deliberated for more than a year and reached a decision without spilling a drop of blood. As James Madison said to the Virginia Ratifying Convention, "Nothing has excited more admiration in the world than the manner in which free governments have been established in America. It was the first instance, from the creation of the world to the American Revolution, that free inhabitants have been seen deliberating on a form of government."

Of course, deliberation of this type and on this broad scale does not simply happen, and it is useful to note the framework that the Founders put in place to enable it. Since tools such as *Robert's Rules of Order* did not yet exist, the Constitutional Convention laid down certain rules at the start of the proceedings. A presiding officer, Nathaniel Gorham of Massachusetts, was chosen to recognize delegates in a queue, making sure no one dominated the discussion or was overlooked. More controversially, the convention decided to do its work behind closed doors. Although Thomas Jefferson was in favor of transparency and openness, a decision was reached that confidentiality would encourage the delegates to speak their minds and change their opinions without the day-to-day pressure of the press or their constituents hovering over every word.

Deliberation was also enhanced by the presentation of alternative plans for the Constitution by some of the state delegations. For example, whereas the convention had been called for the more limited purpose of amending the Articles of Confederation, delegates from Virginia put forward a plan that raised far more fundamental questions about the nature of the federal government and its powers. In a vital sense, the very limited Articles of Confederation, with their requirement of virtual consensus before action, ended up discouraging both deliberation and action by the federal government. The Virginia Plan moved from outcome to process, sort of reversing Machiavelli to say that the means justifies the end, for it is in the protection of the means, and not simply the outcome, that liberty is secured. Instead of relying on mechanical devices of the Articles such as super majorities, it proposed bicameralism, the separation of powers, and veto powers to encourage the emergence of a deliberate sense of the community. The hope was that the Virginia Plan would stimulate both deliberation and action.

Indeed, delegates to the convention were, early on, invited to consider the Virginia Plan, an Amended Virginia Plan, the New Jersey Plan, and the Hamilton Plan, all over the course of about three weeks. That very process of openly examining several approaches to issues both enhanced and encouraged deliberation. For example, James Madison sought a Council of Revision to consider the worthiness of a proposal before it became a law. Although that was voted down, the presidential veto power over policy and a Supreme Court power of judicial review became different ways of accomplishing some of the same goals. Similarly, Madison sought a congressional review over state laws but again lost the vote. With that defeat, however, came a concession: the supremacy clause. The Virginia Plan proposed that Congress would take on those activities for which the states were deemed to be incompetent. Again, the Virginians lost, but a concession listed eighteen powers of Congress. So unlike Nancy Pelosi and Mitch McConnell gathering their troops in secret to win a quick vote, Madison, the father of the Constitution, was content to see his ideas deliberated and even defeated for the good of the whole. Deliberation requires a commitment to the process, not just to one's preferred outcome.

Madison and the Virginians were not the only ones advancing ideas for deliberation at the convention. The New Jersey Plan argued for each state to have one vote in the legislature, rather than proportional representation. If there were to be two bodies in a bicameral legislature, Roger Sherman wanted the states to be represented in one branch and was willing to go along with Madison's proposal that the people be represented in the other. South Carolina and Georgia complicated matters by requesting that wealth, in the form of slave property, be represented. As part of the deliberative process, a committee was formed consisting of one representative from each state to propose a compromise. As a consequence, each state was given representation in one house of Congress, with proportional representation of the people in the other, and three-fifths of the slaves were counted in determining the size of districts. There was fierce debate, and further compromise, but the Great Compromise carried the day. The modern devices that never lead to compromise—because the votes are already counted—would have been entirely foreign to the Founders.

The ratifiers themselves were engaged in deliberation at thirteen separate ratifying conventions to decide whether to approve the proposed new Constitution. But the deliberative process, as was seen in ratification, is rarely a smooth ride or an easy path. By their own ground rules, nine of the thirteen state ratifying conventions needed to approve the new Constitution for it to be adopted. Several state delegations were in a quandary, and the outcome was far from certain. In the end, a series of compromises, which is a hallmark of deliberation, began to move things toward approval. Massachusetts, for example, was persuaded to ratify now and amend later. A number of delegates who were dug in on the idea of a Bill of Rights accepted a promise to review those later in the form of constitutional amendments. But this ratification process ultimately modeled what we sought in the new government: deliberation, through discussion, debate, compromise, and amendment. This is the legacy of deliberation they trusted would be brought forward into the government itself.

In particular the Bill of Rights constituted an important element in the deliberation, reminding us of the restraining nature of the Constitution. On one hand, some felt that the Constitution created too much federal power in comparison with the Articles of Confederation and insisted on a Bill of Rights to limit federal control. On the other hand were those who felt such a listing of rights was unnecessary and even potentially dangerous if it prompted the conclusion that these were all the rights left to the people. In the end, the compromise was not to include a Bill of Rights in the main body of the Constitution, but to leave them for the first Congress to address as a series of amendments, making the first ten amendments a Bill of Rights. All this deliberation also performed an educational purpose, instructing and informing Americans of the limits of federal power and the restraining nature of the Constitution.

Doubtless no one at the Constitutional Convention found the outcome of these debates to be perfect. Delegates at various points failed to show up for votes or walked out. Three declined to sign. But Benjamin Franklin captured the outcome of the deliberative process, which was not perfect but did create "a more perfect" union. Real deliberation requires faith that the sum of everyone's participation will be different from any one person's views but better overall—and more likely to be accepted. This is yet another founding principle that is absent in legislating today.

The effect of the deliberation is evidenced in part by the fact that minds and votes were changed over the question of ratification. For example, the expected vote in Massachusetts going into the ratification process was "no," at 178 to 177, but the final vote was "yes," at 187 to 168. Minds were changed and, therefore, also the outcome. New Hampshire and Virginia both appeared to be deadlocked going in, but following deliberation, ratification was approved in each place. An even more dramatic change took place in New York, where the projected vote was 46 to 19 against ratification, but the final tally was 30 to 27 in favor.[1]

Finally, it is instructive to note how the Founders responded when they lost. Did the deliberative spirit break down into rancor and splits? No: when their side won, they did not boast but were gracious, and when they lost, they did not launch wars of reprisal. Patrick Henry set the tone for this when, after losing the ratification vote in Virginia, it is said that he told his colleagues that he would act "in a constitutional way" and that they should "cherish the new government" and "give it fair play." He told his fellow Antifederalists that it was time to "go home" and work within the newly adopted Constitution.

Deliberation Out of Doors: Further Ratification Debate and *The Federalist Papers*

The four hot months indoors at the Philadelphia convention were hardly the end of the deliberation over the Constitution and a new form of government. The signing of the Constitution by the delegates to the convention on September 17, 1787, merely sent it forward to Congress, which, in turn, dispatched it to the thirteen states for their own ratification deliberation and decision. And so launched an unprecedented public debate, out of doors, through speeches, essays, newspaper articles, tracts, sermons, and everyday conversations. There was deliberation everywhere.

Most prominently, a public debate emerged between the Antifederalists and the Federalists, captured in newspaper essays penned under pseudonyms. The latter essays have since been collected as *The Federalist*, or *The Federalist Papers*. The opening paragraph of *Federalist* No. 1, published on October 27, 1787, set the deliberative agenda in a powerful way:

> After full experience of the insufficiency of the existing federal government, you are invited to deliberate upon a new Constitution. . . . It has been frequently remarked, that it seems to have been reserved to the people of this country to decide, by their conduct and example, the important question, whether societies of men are really capable or not, of establishing good government from reflection and choice, or whether they are forever destined to depend, for their political constitutions, on accident and force. If there be any truth in the remark, the crisis at which we are arrived may, with propriety, be regarded as the period when that decision is to be made; and a wrong election of the part we shall act may, in this view, deserve to be considered as the general misfortune of mankind.

A brief walk through *The Federalist* underscores the importance and the nature of deliberation in these out-of-doors essays and discussions. We already know about *Federalist* No. 63 and the Founders' quest for "the cool and deliberate sense of the community," and also *Federalist* No. 71 and its "republican principle" that "the deliberate sense of the community should govern." But in the eighty-five essays of *The Federalist* one finds some fifty references to deliberation. *Federalist* No. 78, for example, refers to democracy's self-connecting mechanism based upon "better information and more deliberate reflection." Those participating in the Constitutional Convention were themselves of the people's "deliberate choice" (*Federalist* No. 38). In the end, the goal is "the regular deliberations and decisions of a respectable majority" (*Federalist* No. 22).

The authors of *The Federalist* essays also discussed "the circumstances favorable to deliberation" (*Federalist* No. 68) as well as obstacles to effective deliberation. The presence of faction, Alexander Hamilton wrote in *Federalist* No. 15, is a "poison in the deliberations of all bodies of men." Especially damaging to deliberation, Hamilton continued, is getting in a hurry to pass legislation. "In the legislature, promptitude of decision is oftener an evil more than a benefit," Hamilton wrote in *Federalist* No. 70, adding that "differences of opinion and the jarrings of parties . . . often promote deliberation and circumspection, and serve to check excesses in the majority."

The debates between the Federalists and the Antifederalists played out intensely across several states for a year, yet no one declared war. The Antifederalists argued that the proposed new federal government would have too much power and leave too little power to the states. They debated whether the new government should be federal, national, or, in the end, a blend of the two. There were clashes over the roles of all the branches of government, as well as how they would be constructed and operate. A key question was whether a Bill of Rights was a necessary part of the Constitution; it was added later. So these debates were over the most fundamental issues and they were heated and intense. Yet they also constituted a fruitful and extended deliberation from which a number of compromises were ultimately drawn.

Structures for Deliberation: A Constitutional Legacy

While the Founders were busy practicing and teaching deliberation in the outdoor debates over the Constitution, they also threaded into the document itself a series of structures and processes that would protect and enhance deliberation in the government. Unfortunately, many of these devices are today thought of as antiquated or obstructionist, preventing the government from moving speedily in the direction this or that faction would like it to go. But in fact, in the spirit of Hamilton's argument in *Federalist* No. 70, their real purpose was to slow down a rush to this or that legislative enactment to allow for a full and mature deliberation. As Jeffrey Rosen, head of the National Constitution Center, has said, they were a kind of cooling mechanism.[2] Although today many on the left view the Constitution as an empowering document, and those on the right see it as restraining, it is in fact a nuanced document with elements of both.

A survey of the Constitution reveals a number of structures established to enhance deliberation. In Article I, Section 1, for example, bicameralism, or two houses of the legislature, not just one, is established. In Section 2, age and other requirements are stated for members of the legislature, enabling a more mature deliberation. Senators, in Section 3, have staggered elections and longer terms, leading to the likelihood of enhanced experience and deliberation. Section 3 also provides an elaborate deliberative process for impeachment. In Section 6 there are personal protections for those engaged in debate in Congress. Even Section 9's prohibition against titles of nobility can be seen as equalizing participants in legislative deliberation.

In Article II, the electoral process clearly takes the election of the president out of the realm of direct democracy and into a more complex and deliberative process. The requirement in Section 3 that the president give a State of the Union message to the legislature facilitates deliberation. Article VII provides for a fulsome deliberative process in the ratification of the Constitution, while Article V establishes an elaborate process for the consideration and passage of amendments to the Constitution.

These constitutional structures to enhance deliberation are explicated and defended throughout *The Federalist* essays. In *Federalist* No. 9, for example, Hamilton noted improvements made in the science of politics that were unknown to the ancients but that would allow for better deliberation and improved governance in the American republic. The regular distribution of power into distinct departments; the introduction of legislative balances and checks; the institution of the courts composed of judges holding their offices during good behavior; the representation of the people in the legislature by deputies of their own election: these are, as Hamilton said, either wholly new discoveries or have made their principal progress in modern times. And they largely serve the purpose of broadening and enhancing the deliberative process, requiring both chambers of the legislature and the executive to be involved in consideration and adoption of laws, adding the courts into the review. The separation of powers, bicameralism, and the independent judiciary are all improvements in the science of government that increase deliberation.

James Madison pointed out another such improvement in the next essay, *Federalist* No. 10, further elaborated in *Federalist* No. 14: the enlarged orbit of the republic. Whereas the ancients thought republican ideas only worked well in a small republic, Madison said we have learned it is just the opposite. In a large republic, the clashing and jarring of different interest groups and views will both enhance deliberation and prevent one or another faction from running ahead to secure its successful adoption of a policy or bill. *Federalist* No. 10 also made the important argument that the way to deal with faction in a republic—which Madison thought was inherent in the nature of man—is to pit one faction against another in an enlarged republic or, as Madison so eloquently stated it, rely on ambition to counteract ambition.

Faction is so dangerous to deliberation because it is a form of war. It is one group, perhaps even a majority, arming itself to overpower the preferences, interests, and rights of others. What the Founders felt was needed was the ability of the people and their elected representatives to talk and work things through.

We will not always have enlightened leaders—or enlightened citizens, for that matter—so we need processes and structures to require that the conversation be carried forward in a mature, deliberative manner. Again, these are the separations of powers, checks and balances, federalism, bicameral legislature, and independent judiciary, all there to keep the deliberation going and not have things settled too easily or quickly in favor of any faction. The point is that public policy should be made through deliberation, not war.

Then, too, citizens deliberated in contexts beyond just voting. New England town meetings were the most obvious examples of this in which the people participated in local governance. These descendants of the Greek city-states were a regular part of civic life in the early colonies of New England. But sermons in churches in the colonial period also engaged members in reflection on political matters, as did newspapers, pamphlets, and other speeches. This sort of local deliberation, which is rare today, was assumed by the Founders to be part of the fabric of civic life and a complement to the formal deliberations in the seats of government.

The Purpose of Deliberation: Enlightened Consent of the Governed

All this deliberation, however, is not for its own sake. Public deliberation is to make policy through the enlightened consent of the people. As the Declaration of Independence stated,

"Governments are instituted among Men, deriving their just powers from the consent of the governed." The whole basis of a government's legitimacy comes from the consent of its people, and deliberation is vital to gathering, agreeing upon, and stating that consent. As Alexander Hamilton put it in *Federalist* No. 22, "The fabric of American empire ought to rest on the basis of the consent of the people. The stream of national power ought to flow immediately from that pure original fountain of all legitimate authority."

Historically regimes had not relied upon consent of the governed to establish their legitimacy and exercise their authority. More common than the consent of the people was simply the people's obedience to their government. In a critical sense, then, the American republic was based on an agreed movement from serfdom to freedom, from people being subject to their government to the people consenting to the rule of their government. Such freedom would not be without its problems, but the Founders sought to deliberate toward a solution. If government by consent was to be the hardware of the American republic, deliberation would be the software that actually allowed it to work.

How, then, would the people express their consent? The first expression of consent comes through voting in elections. The Founders considered a whole range of questions about elections that would define the nature of this form of consent. For example, how often should elections be held? On one hand, more frequent elections would keep the consent of the people closer at hand, but some stability in the government would also be needed. Does everyone have a right to vote, or is there an age of consent? If we want enlightened consent, should there be any rules about intelligence, or a citizenship test? Should voting be based upon gender, property ownership, or other considerations? So enlightened consent was the principle, but the details would change over time with the mores and understandings of the society.

Then the question arises whether representatives elected by the people are bound to carry out what the people want done or whether elected officials are free, even responsible, to exercise their own judgment. In other words, do only the people deliberate in choosing a representative, or do the elected officials also deliberate? The Antifederalist view is that elected officials were mere agents, responsible directly to the electorate to carry out their will. But the Federalists believed that officials were sent into government to deliberate: to be statesmen with loyalty to their constituency, to be sure, but also loyalty to the nation, to their body, and to the process of legislating and governing. As political philosopher Willmoore Kendall rightly said, members of Congress take part in a continuing dialectical relationship with their constituents.[3]

One could well ask whether finding the consent of the governed is still an objective of policy making today. In his first inaugural address as president, Ronald Reagan said that government had grown so much that it "shows signs of having grown beyond the consent of the governed." Changing fundamental systems such as health care on the basis of narrow, party-line votes hardly seems like a search for the consent of the governed. The country would do well to return to the Founders' central objective: deliberating to find the consent of the governed.

Enemies of Deliberation

Since we argue that modern policy makers have largely disavowed the deliberative track in favor of emergency actions and war, perhaps we should examine the founding era to see what dangers and enemies its leaders saw to deliberation. Did the Founders foresee some of the very challenges we are now experiencing? And if so, were they able to suggest any antidotes to these problems and propose ways to stay on the deliberative track?

When the Founders said the goal was to identify and follow "the cool and deliberate sense of the community" over time, clearly one enemy of that process was thought to be intemperate, hot, or rushed action by government leaders. As Hamilton said in *Federalist* No. 70, hurry in the legislative process "is oftener an evil more than a benefit" because it silences voices and disagreements that allow for a more thorough deliberation and a better outcome. By contrast, the Founders constantly called for moderation in the deliberative process. James Madison, in *Federalist* No. 37, decried "that public measures are rarely investigated with that spirit of moderation, which is essential to a just estimate of their real tendency to advance, or obstruct, the public good." Indeed, Madison summarized the battle between immoderation and deliberation quite well when he wrote in *Federalist* No. 42, "[T]he mild voice of reason, pleading the cause of an enlarged and permanent interest, is but too often drowned, before public bodies as well as individuals, by the clamors of an impatient avidity for immediate and immoderate gain." These words sound very familiar to us today, especially when legislators hide the language of their bills to the last minute and carefully arrange limited debates and party-line votes.

The Senate, in particular, was proposed as a moderating chamber that would further prevent intemperate action. George Washington is said to have told Thomas Jefferson that, just as he had a saucer to cool hot coffee, so a Senate would cool the passions of the House. As Madison said in *Federalist* No. 62, "The necessity of a senate is not less indicated by the propensity of all single and numerous assemblies, to yield to the impulse of sudden and violent passions, and to be seduced by factious leaders into intemperate and pernicious resolutions." Indeed, the composition of the smaller Senate, and its several rules and practices, would all contribute to a measured process of deliberation. Until this was changed to a direct election of the people by the Seventeenth Amendment in 1913, members of the Senate were actually elected by a different constituency: the states themselves. Some argue that, with the elimination of this additional filter, the Senate more often falls in line with the rushed party-line votes of the House, as opposed to standing as a very different kind of body providing a distinctive cool, deliberative process.

Another way the Founders described this problem in deliberation concerned the difference between passions or interests on one hand and opinions on the other hand. Broadly speaking, passions of men are not regulated by reason and are, therefore, not helpful to deliberation; whereas opinions are reached through a rational process and are subject to discussion and deliberation. This distinction is drawn in several places in *The Federalist*, especially Nos. 10, 41, and 49. In No. 41, for example, Madison referred to "the passions of the unthinking and . . . the prejudices of the misthinking" over and against "cool and candid people [who] at once reflect." Madison concluded, "[I]t is the reason alone, of the public, that ought to control and regulate the government. The passions ought to be controlled and regulated by the government" (*Federalist* No. 49).

All these smaller enemies of deliberation led to what the Founders thought was the big one: faction, including majority faction. Factions marshal their opinions and interests and go to war, seeking only to win the day. Madison and his colleagues saw a lot of those at the state level between the American Revolution and the adoption of the Constitution, and he elaborated on it in his classic piece *Federalist* No. 10. In that eloquent essay, Madison described a faction as a group "united and actuated by the common impulse of passion, or of interest, adverse to the right of other citizens, or to the permanent and aggregate interests of the community." As scholar Joseph M. Bessette rightly observed, "Defusing majority faction was the first step in establishing representative institutions capable of sound political deliberation."[4]

Actually defusing majority faction proved difficult then, as it does now. Madison's thesis, articulated in *Federalist* No. 10, was that one could either remove the causes of faction or control its effects. Removing the cause was problematic, Madison wrote, because doing so would entail the abolition of liberty, which the Constitution sought to protect. Further, Madison wrote, "the latent causes of faction are . . . sown in the nature of man." More promising than relying on the virtue of the people, he felt, was to manage the effects of faction by refining and enlarging the public views in a large republic so that ambition, or faction, would counteract ambition. This, of course, could hardly be undertaken in a pure or direct democracy, but was possible in a republic with its various structures and tools of refinement. Nevertheless, it seems fair to say that even today many of the wars and the gridlock in politics that people find so disheartening result from factions warring against factions, seeking narrow party-line votes so that their bare majorities may prevail.

The Founders recognized that there might be emergencies, especially in times of war, when the sort of careful and lengthy deliberation they preferred no longer made sense. As Madison acknowledged in *Federalist* No. 45, "The operations of the federal government will be most extensive and important in times of war and danger." But one obvious danger was whether the government would reduce its power following a war and return to normal deliberative processes. Although this was done, for example, in the "return to normalcy" following World War I, it did not happen following World War II. A less obvious problem has been the ability of presidents and legislators to turn all kinds of domestic challenges into wars: the war on poverty, war on drugs, war on crime, etc., thereby justifying less deliberation and more federal power in those areas.

In short, the Founders identified several problems w
taining a deliberative democracy: hot and intemperate a
seeks to limit deliberation; passions and interests that c
ject themselves to reason; factions, especially majority factions,
that go to war to accomplish their aims over the good of the republic; and war powers that limit deliberation but never return
to normal, and even grow as new domestic priorities are declared
to be emergencies or matters of war. All of these and more afflict
the republic today in ways that limit and even defy governing by
the cool, deliberate sense of the community over time.

The Future of Deliberation

The Founders were rightly proud of the fact that whereas all
previous governments had been established through force or
fraud, the American republic was formed through consent and
deliberation to preserve liberty. Moreover, they framed a Constitution that sought to maintain deliberation through various
checks and balances and separations of power we have come to
call respectively federalism and republicanism. In fact, political
scientist Leslie Lipson points out that federalism has been "the
greatest of American contributions to the art of government."[5]
Indeed, the American Constitution is both an empowering document and a restraining document. Both the Founders' example
of deliberation and the structures of deliberation established in
the Constitution are valuable legacies for making public policy
today.

But these legacies of deliberation are under threat. Whereas deliberation and consent came in the front door of the American republic, force and fraud (what we call war) are always lurking and ready to come in the back door. The powers of force and fraud, including emergency and war, came to the fore during the New Deal of the 1930s and have only grown over time, accompanied now by calls to weaken the Founders' protections. Maintaining a government of deliberation has become more challenging, not less, with the rise of executive power and the modern presidency.

We do not go back to the founding to propose that America must remain there. But at the same time, changing public policy and certainly altering the Constitution require deliberation. In the case of the Constitution, the amendment process demands extensive deliberation at both the federal and state levels, with the requirements of a two-thirds vote of both houses of Congress and a vote of three-fourths of the state legislatures. And in a sense, change requires a deliberation between the past and the present, understanding how and why the Founders established the various protections that are in place and how changes will affect all the many interests at stake. As we have seen, this sort of purposeful deliberation, continuing to seek the cool, deliberate sense of the community, has become increasingly rare. Whether it can be recovered or refreshed, or whether it needs to be reinvented for a new time, becomes a challenge for present and future generations.

Critical departures from the Founders' view of deliberative democracy have been made over the past hundred years. These departures from the roots of the American regime are based in an unenlightened rejection of the Founders' view of deliberative democracy and a new understanding that the preeminent values of the regime are equality and action rather than liberty and deliberation. The concept of deliberation came to be seen in the progressive era, the New Deal era, and the latter part of the twentieth century as undesirable or unnecessary. The Founders saw deliberation as essential for the defense of popular government, which defense placed the public good and personal liberty at the apex of values. "Action" and "mobilization" rather than "reflection" and "choice" seem to be the appealing words these days. Along the way, the claim that the founding was democratic, in the sense of being of, by, and for the people, has also been criticized. In fact, the rejection of deliberation is in many ways grounded in the proposition that the founding was undemocratic—and deliberately opposed to action, period.

These rejections of the Founders' approach are major causes of the twenty-first-century crisis in governance. All the more reason, we say, to retrieve the understanding of deliberative democracy at the founding to come back to the present and face the future state of deliberative democracy better informed.

To formulate the two dimensions of deliberative democracy slightly differently: the "depravity" of human beings means that we must pay attention to institutional arrangements; the "virtue" of human beings is needed to make the experiment defensible. If we learn nothing else from the American founding, it is that in the end it is the character of the people and the quality of the institutions that are the keys to the success or failure of the

American experiment. The people choose their representatives, and the hope is that they will select delegates who are also wise and virtuous. And a critical number of representatives can and should willingly change their minds when presented with reasonable arguments, and the hope is that they will do so without suing or pouting or rioting or undermining or killing or emigrating or lying because the result is not to their liking. There is something about the process of deliberation in a popular government rather than simply a purely democratic outcome per se that commends our allegiance to deliberative democracy.

Not everybody has to be deliberatively inclined for deliberative democracy to work. After all, as Madison said, "enlightened statesmen will not always be at the helm." Madison also recognized a certain "depravity" in human nature. But there have to be (1) a sufficient number of citizens who have public virtue and practical wisdom and (2) a sufficient number of decent and responsible representatives who will follow the high ground example. There must also be (3) a disposition in "We the people" to accept the result of deliberation. And (4) following Madison, the institutional framework of checks and balances and the separation of powers must provide the auxiliary precautions when the people and their representatives temporarily stray or the electorate has voters' remorse.

NOTES

1. See http://teachingamericanhistory.org/ratification/overview/.

2. Taylor Lorenz, "James Madison Would Be Horrified by a Tweeting President," *The Atlantic,* June 25, 2018.

3. John Alvis, "Willmoore Kendall and the Demise of Congressional Deliberation," *The Intercollegiate Review* 23, no. 2 (Spring 1988): 59.

4. Joseph M. Bessette, *The Mild Voice of Reason* (Chicago: University of Chicago Press, 1994), 16.

5. Leslie Lipson, *The Democratic Civilization* (New York: Oxford University Press 1964), 14.

5 How to Manage the War Metaphor in Public Policy

THE WAY FORWARD

American politics and government have evolved into a state of constant wars and emergencies. The nation lives under nearly thirty formally declared states of national emergency, with their increased executive powers, spending, and regulation. All manner of wars that presidents have declared against domestic problems since the 1960s continue to be fought: wars on poverty, crime, drugs, terror, and the like. Within the government itself, war has become the primary metaphor for action. President Trump sees the courts at war with his priorities, as one branch battles against another. Even within the branches, especially Congress, the parties are in a constant state of warfare against one another.

Deliberation, which the Founders saw as the way government should conduct its business, is largely gone. The US Senate, for example—long acknowledged as the greatest deliberative body in the world—hardly deliberates anymore. No longer subject to lengthy committee processes to study, debate, and amend legislation, bills are held in secret by the majority party until sufficient votes are available for passage and then rushed onto the floor for a vote. Major pieces of legislation, such as the Affordable Care Act, are not compromised to achieve bipartisan support, but instead are passed on a pure party-line vote. Presidents, frustrated by gridlock and warfare in Congress, increasingly turn to executive orders to accomplish their goals.

Before discussing what solutions might be proposed for this state of affairs, we must first identify the nature of the problem. As Albert Einstein said, "If I had an hour to solve a problem and my life depended on it, I would spend the first fifty-five minutes determining the proper question to ask, for once I know the proper question, I could solve the problem in less than five minutes." Of course, we are not as smart as Einstein, and it would take us more than five minutes to propose a solution to this problem of war in public policy, but we agree that it is crucial to first identify the question, or the nature of the problem.

Conventional wisdom suggests that the underlying problem is one of polarization, at least among our political leaders if not among the people themselves. Americans are hopelessly divided, the argument goes, and that division has shown up in government, resulting in gridlock. There is some support for this thesis, although there is more evidence of polarization and gridlock among our political leaders than among the people themselves.

Yes, there is polarization at the top, in government. And yes, there are problems, if not outright polarization, among the people. But what is little focused on, yet important, is the set of filters, or moderating influences, that used to exist between the government and the people. We believe those filters are clogged and those institutions have faded in such a way that the probability of war and emergency in our political life has greatly increased and the prospect for deliberation correspondingly diminished. We illustrate and better understand this by analogy to Plato's famous "divided line."

The Divided Line

In *The Republic*, Plato illustrated two distinct worlds and the "divided line" that separates them. Above the line, where philosophers such as Plato sought to live, is the metaphysical world. There one lives the life of the mind, unencumbered by the temptations of the body. Meanwhile, the rest of us live in a physical world, which Plato described as a world of shadows and factions, in contrast to the higher levels of reality of the metaphysical realm. Whereas most of us are consigned to live in a lower-level material world where things can be seen but not thought, the philosopher lives in the world of higher ideals where things unseen are nevertheless thought.

Like all analogies or metaphors, ours is imperfect, but we think of the American republic as operating above and below a divided line. In the highest sense, the Founders placed the Constitution and its ideals at the top of the realm. Its foundational and enduring principles are what make the republic work: the separation of powers, bicameralism, an independent judiciary, frequent and regular elections, and so forth. Also above the line, in our understanding, are the political leaders who are seeking to implement those ideals. Of course, we understand that politicians may be closer to Plato's earthly kings than heavenly philosophers, but let us imagine them above the line for now, seeking to accomplish the Constitution's noble purposes.

Below the institutional and social line we have drawn, live the people. In the beginning of the republic there were 3 million people, now there are nearly 330 million people. They form and join interest groups and seek in all manner of ways to have their voices heard above the line. By all accounts, they are frustrated with government above the line and do not feel their voice is being heard and heeded. One survey concluded that only 19 percent of the American people believe the federal government has the consent of the governed.[1] Of course, when you have one federal representative for 60,000 people at the founding and 1 per nearly 760,000 persons today, it is little surprise that there is a huge strain to accomplish the sort of deliberation and representation the Founders intended and the people desire.

Since the United States was intended to be a representative, not a pure, democracy, a good deal of filtering and moderating was expected at the line itself. A free press, protected by the First Amendment, was an important vehicle for debate and communication. Soon enough, political parties developed, allowing interests to sort and organize to be better heard and to win elections. As Alexis de Tocqueville described in his nineteenth-century *Democracy in America*, all manner of civic associations, churches, and informal groupings were a very active part of the social and political scene. All these filtering and moderating devices would assist traffic in crossing the line between the people and their elected representatives. Such filters refine the flow, eliminating sludge and facilitating the flow of good ideas.

By now, however, the filters have become clogged and many have quit serving their purposes altogether. While sociologists and other social scientists study what has gone wrong with the people such that our republic is not working well, and while government reformers seek mechanical and rules-based changes in Washington, DC, we believe further attention needs to be given to the Madisonian travel back and forth at the divided line itself.

Filters at the Line Are No Longer Working

The Founders believed in a filtered democracy, not a direct democracy. They clearly understood that one of the strengths and challenges of a representative government was establishing a robust flow of information and communication between the people and their government. James Madison noted in *Federalist* No. 10 that a primary purpose of representative government was "to refine and enlarge the public views, by passing them through the medium of a chosen body of citizens, whose wisdom may best discern the true interest of their country." Representative government, then, was itself intended to filter and moderate the views of the people so that they would be comprehensible to government and actionable as appropriate. The Founders believed that frequent elections allowed the filter to clean itself and remain effective. Nothing was more important at the line than elections, allowing the voters to express their consent.

We would argue that as the size of the republic grew, it became important to have additional filtering and moderating devices to enable that flow of information to take place. In 1787, there was one representative in Congress for 60,000 people, with a constitutional ideal of one for 30,000. Congress took on the responsibility for adjusting the number of representatives to the increase and movement of the people but, in the early 1900s, Congress limited the number of representatives to 435, where it remains. So now we have moved from an ideal of 1 representative for 30,000 to 1 for nearly 760,000, a major challenge indeed for a representative democracy, putting a strain on the entire system.

Election reforms are always in the air, but they never really solve the problem. Gerrymandering of districts, campaign finance reform, and voting reform are all hot topics these days, but the record of success is not strong. For example, a few years ago California moved to a "top two" primary method of voting, in which the top two vote getters in the primary, regardless of political party, advance to the general election. The hope— that this would lead to more moderate candidates and elected officials—has not been realized, and unintended (or perhaps intended) consequences of races with two final candidates from the same party are relatively common, actually reducing voter choice. Campaign finance reform seems to plug certain holes in the law, but only until lawyers find new holes in the revised laws.

In the end, little seems to change, so we doubt that election reform is the key to saving the republic.

Freedom of the press, guaranteed by the First Amendment, reminds us that the media should be one important filter between the people and their government. Yet with the explosion of mass and social media channels and providers, most taking up one side or another on public issues, people find themselves gorged on too much unfiltered information. People consume the medium that best reflects and reinforces their own views, following channels such as Fox News or MSNBC, for example, that offer alternate versions of reality rather than all sides of complex policy issues. President Trump has joined in by attacking the press directly, claiming that the media now offer "fake news," further encouraging conspiracy theories linked to war. These dueling and clashing views of politics and policy reinforce the war metaphor in public policy rather than creating opportunities for civil debate and thoughtful deliberation at the line. In particular, social media stir up passions rather than fostering any sort of rational deliberation.

In a way not foreseen in the founding era, attorneys have added filters between the government and the people, sometimes taking up where the press has let down. If the people are not receiving adequate information from their government, for example, lawyers will file a Freedom of Information Act request to require a government agency to release pertinent information. If people believe the government may be acting improperly, perhaps discriminating against them, lawyers will be called upon to bring legal action against the government. If there is a secret above the line, you can be sure lawyers at the line will try to sniff it out and share it with the people.

Political parties, which should be useful filters at the line, have increasingly become warriors at the political battlefront instead. Although it is sometimes suggested that the Founders did not really know about or anticipate the role of political parties, the evidence suggests otherwise. In *The Federalist* No. 10, for example, Madison expressed considerable concern about faction and people falling into warring groups. The Constitutional Convention, as well as the state ratifying conventions, saw various factions emerging—ultimately two prominent ones, the Federalists and the Antifederalists were essentially political parties—but they were able to resolve their differences through deliberation. *The Federalist* is full of references to faction, including majority and minority factions, if not to political parties directly.

Until the 1970s, political parties operated largely on a state and local basis and were often effective as filtering devices. People not only could vote themselves, but they also joined parties and other interest groups, both to learn about issues and candidates and to seek to influence the outcome of elections. But from the 1970s on, the national parties grew dramatically in influence and are, by now, part of the warlike system, effectively dictating policies to state and local candidates, funding candidates (sometimes even in primaries), threatening to oppose incumbents who do not support their stance on issues, and so forth.[2] The nationalization and standardization of political parties have greatly reduced their effectiveness as filters at the line, helping to engage people in civic and political life.

When the French journalist and philosopher Alexis de Tocqueville visited America in 1831, he was most impressed by the variety and influence of civic associations on the body politic. Tocqueville observed,

> Americans of all conditions, all ages, all minds constantly unite. Not only do they have commercial and industrial associations in which all take part, but they also have a thousand other kinds: religious, moral, grave, futile, very general and very particular, immense and very small. . . . There is nothing . . . that does more to attract our regard than the intellectual and moral associations of America.[3]

These civic associations were understood by Tocqueville to play an important role in moderating what he saw as one of the young democracy's dangers, excessive individualism, and to help develop the virtue of the people, thought by the Founders (*Federalist* No. 55) to be essential for self-government.

Like the free press, however, civic associations today are less able to play their valuable moderating role at the line. Sociologist Robert Putnam, in his book *Bowling Alone* (2000), argued that Americans have indeed become selfish and have withdrawn from participation in civic associations such as bowling leagues and Elks Clubs. Others, such as David Davenport and Hanna Skandera, have argued that civic associations have changed in nature, albeit in ways that nevertheless harm their traditional role of generating and moderating civic engagement.[4] Davenport and Skandera argue persuasively that many traditional civic associations now spend a great deal of their time lobbying the government and dealing with government regulation, rather than encouraging the practice and development of civic participation. Many newer civic associations are NGOs (nongovernmental organizations) and other forms of advocacy organizations. Unlike those of Tocqueville's day, these civic associations are players in the policy wars rather than groups that moderate and filter at the line between the people and their government. Similarly, think tanks have proliferated, but they tend to be more advocates than thinkers.

Civic associations—which might include anything from chambers of commerce to labor unions, from scouting organizations to churches, from lobbying organizations to action groups—should play a robust dual function at the line. First, they should be engaging people directly in civic activity of all kinds, both for the problems that can be solved for the society as well as for the training the members receive in so doing. Second, when appropriate to the type of organization, they may also serve as go-betweens, influencers, between the people and their government. Lobbying is not inappropriate for civic associations, but it should not be the full extent of what they do.

Although one could place federalism in many places on the divided line diagram, we choose to locate it at the line as an additional filter between the federal government and the people. In this case, we think primarily of federalism as keeping as many government decisions as possible close to the people, whether at the local, regional, or state level. Of course, the Tenth Amendment establishes this sort of federalism explicitly: "The powers not delegated to the United States by the Constitution . . . are reserved to the States, respectively, or to the people." Localism engages the people most directly in self-government, such as serving on school boards, participating in town hall meetings, or volunteering on community projects.

Unfortunately, recent decades have seen a steady encroachment by the federal government on state and local power. In a nationalized and now global economy, more business practices need to be regulated centrally, or so Washington says. Education, through the No Child Left Behind law of the George W. Bush years, was shifted from a state and local matter to an increasingly federal one. Health care under President Barack Obama became a federal mandate. Congress used its spending power to pressure states into following federal speed limit standards on highways. The Supreme Court said more federal power was justified by the growth of interstate commerce, not to mention the due process and equal protection clauses of the Fourteenth Amendment. If not clogged up, the state and local filters at the line have been significantly weakened by the growth of federal power.

Some of these clogged and ineffective filters are more easily repaired than others. Removing the stranglehold of political parties on the policy process is important but difficult work. Yet there are signs of hope. Many Americans, especially millennials, see the need for a third political party that might break the logjam. Increasingly voters, again especially young people, are registering as independents or "decline to state," indicating their lack of identification with the two major parties. Perhaps a state such as California, where independents nearly outnumber Republicans, might find a way to a new moderate/independent form of politics.

The state of the media also seems difficult to repair. Initially the proliferation of new media outlets—cable and satellite television, Internet and social media—seemed like a promising way to break up the monopoly that a few key television networks and newspapers held over news content and presentation. And, indeed, one can find seemingly every point of view under the sun somewhere in the vast media wasteland. But increasingly the media take partisan points of view on politics rather than even trying to provide citizens objective information so that they may reach their own well-informed views. When it comes to strident voices conducting wars over politics and policy, the media have clearly become part of the problem, not part of the solution, and viewers seem to accept it.

Progressives have a different answer to the clogged-up filters at the line—get rid of the filters altogether, they say. Whereas the Founders deliberately constructed a filtered democracy, progressives prefer a direct democracy that would do away with the filters. For one, they say, do away with the Electoral College, passing a "national popular vote" bill in many progressive states so that eventually their state electoral votes would go to the winner of the national popular vote. Progressive academics put forward even bolder prescriptions. The US Senate is undemocratic, they say, and needs reform, its membership restructured.[5] If gridlock is the problem, and it is they say, eliminating obstructionist checks and balances is the answer. Progressives argue, as they long have, for America to turn toward a parliamentary system to escape the roadblocks of checks and balances and separations of power.

We join the Founders in saying precisely the opposite: it is the filtered democracy, also called a republic, that allows for the deliberation we need in both society and our government today. We desperately need citizens who are more engaged at the line, whether in civic associations or their local government, deliberating and acting on matters of public policy. We need the media providing balanced information so that citizens may better understand and deliberate on the issues of the day. We need open and contested elections with candidates more strongly committed to the people than to their political parties. The filters need to be unclogged and made to work again on behalf of our representative democracy.

Above the Line: Dysfunction in Washington, DC

Enemies of deliberation are clearly in the ascendancy in our nation's capital. It has become the realm of outcome politics, where the means do not matter, only winning. Two of the Founders' distinctive contributions—federalism and separation of powers—are in decline. Instead, we live in a world of war powers, executive orders, national emergencies, and gridlock. Indeed, public policy in Washington has become war, and the president is the commander in chief. Franklin Roosevelt had threatened this, concluding his first inaugural address, in 1933, by saying that if he did not have sufficient authority to carry out his programs to combat the Great Depression, he would "ask the Congress for the one remaining instrument to meet the crisis—broad Executive power to wage a war against the emergency." Presidents now routinely exercise such power without bothering to ask Congress. This situation must change if we are interested in fixing the filtration system.

Is it fixable? Donald Trump has said "no," that Washington, DC, has become a swamp that he intends to drain. However, Trump's disrupter approach to governing is likely short-term, so the question remains whether there is any longer-term hope for politics and policy to shift away from wars and emergencies to bipartisan deliberation.

As a starting point, it would seem imperative that Congress be dramatically strengthened and improved. As the editor of *National Affairs*, Yuval Levin, has said, "[T]he weakness of the Congress is the foremost problem now confronting our constitutional system."[6] To address that, reformers in Washington, DC, have been wearing a new cap. Patterned after Donald Trump's ubiquitous campaign cap, it changes one important word, proclaiming, "Make Congress Great Again." It reflects both a realization that a key contributor to the dysfunction in Washington is a weakened Congress and a determination that our national legislature might reform its way back to greatness.

How Congress Lost Its Power

By any account, Congress has been in a deep and steady decline in the view of the American people. Its approval ratings range between 10 and 12 percent. More than 41 percent of those polled by YouGov say Congress has accomplished even less than usual lately.[7] By one 2018 tally, the Senate had voted on only 6 non-budgetary amendments so far that year, and a 2018 *Politico* report tallied only 25 roll-call votes on binding amendments in that two-year Congress, compared with 154 at the same point in the previous Congress.[8] Polarization in Congress is up while deliberation is down.

Many members of Congress have been voting with their feet, choosing in near-record numbers to leave Washington rather than run for reelection. Some have explicitly pointed to their frustration with the polarized and dysfunctional nature of Congress. Although he is not leaving Congress, freshman senator John Kennedy (R-LA), commenting on the fact that he had not been able to get a vote on a single proposed amendment in the first fifteen months of his term, said, "I think it sucks."

What has led to the present decline of Congress? One obvious answer is that Congress, once the first of the branches, has lost power and initiative to the presidency. The Founders thought of Congress as the first of the three branches (legislative, executive, and judicial) of government. As James Madison pointed out in *Federalist* No. 51, "In republican government, the legislative authority necessarily prevails." Indeed, the Founders were concerned that there be sufficient "energy" in the executive, and Alexander Hamilton concluded in *Federalist* No. 78 that, with control over neither the purse nor the sword, the judiciary would be the weakest of the branches.

By now, that constitutional order has been turned on its head, with the president and the courts vying for primacy and Congress bringing up the rear. For example, although Article I, Section 8 of the Constitution grants to Congress the power to "declare war," leaving the president to carry out wars as "commander in chief" under Article II, Section 2, Congress has essentially deferred its war powers to the president. The 2018 military attacks on Syria's chemical weapons facilities were ordered by the president with no involvement by Congress. When Congress did authorize the war on terror, it was in 2001, a week after the 9/11 attacks, and that authorization has been stretched by three presidents to cover all kinds of military actions, including some against groups that did not even exist at the time of the authorization.

This shift in the constitutional order of war powers is not due solely to presidential excess, but also to an unwillingness by Congress to step up to its proper role. When Congress had an opportunity to debate the war against ISIS and military action in Syria in 2014, for example, it took a pass and instead adjourned to go home early and campaign. In an election year, members of Congress did not want to take difficult or unpopular votes, with one congressman, Jack Kingston (R-GA), frankly admitting that "a lot of people would like to stay on the sideline and say [to the president], 'Just bomb the place and tell us about it later.'" It is hard to work up a lot of excitement or even sympathy for a Congress that takes a pass on the difficult questions placed squarely on its plate by the Constitution.

Other powers have been shifted away from Congress by the rise of the administrative state and the ever-expanding role of federal agency rule making. In their important 2016 book *Constitutional Morality and the Rise of Quasi-Law*, Bruce P. Frohnen and George W. Carey document Congress's inclination to delegate complex and difficult questions to administrative agencies when they legislate. Congress is now content to pass broad legislation on important subjects such as workplace safety and protection of the environment, leaving the details to be worked out by federal agencies. Of course, the devil is usually in the details, so executive agencies and their "quasi-law" become even more powerful than Congress in many areas. There is, at best, a limited check on the administrative state, which is not designed for deliberation in any event. Columnist George Will has rightly described this weakening of checks and balances as Congress "expelling rather than consolidating power," the opposite problem from what the Founders had feared.[9]

In fact, if one were to summarize the most important powers the Constitution assigned to Congress, all of them are in decline. The power of the purse—which James Madison called in *Federalist* No. 58 "the most complete and effectual weapon with which any constitution can arm the immediate representatives of the people"—is now driven by the executive branch, with its five-hundred-staff Office of Management and Budget. The power over treaties? Now presidents simply sign and unsign international accords of various kinds, or "adopt" them by executive order, as Obama did the Paris Agreement on climate change, rarely bothering to submit a formal treaty for Senate approval. The appointment power? How much does that really mean when a president such as Donald Trump oversees a revolving door cabinet, changing secretaries seemingly at will? Taxation? President Trump feels free to change America's tariff policies with a tweet and a signature. From the war powers on, all of the primary powers of Congress have been weakened, while the president's hand has been strengthened.

The sheer size and scope of the administrative state make it a challenge for Congress to keep up. Kevin R. Kosar, in a K Street Policy study, points out that the executive branch "comprises 180 agencies, 4.1 million civilian and active military employees and a budget of $3.9 trillion per year." By comparison, Congress consists of "a handful of agencies, has 10,000 employees and is funded at $4.3 billion per year." Kosar also examines the relative output, noting that Congress enacts perhaps "50 significant laws each year while executive agencies issue 4,000 new rules per year, with 80 to 100 of these having economic effects of $100 million or more." As Kosar concludes, "A part-time mostly amateur legislature cannot compete with a colossal, full-time executive branch."[10]

We have reached a point where one wonders whether the very role of Congress itself has been radically transformed. Nelson Polsby, a longtime observer of Congress, argued that the US Congress was a "transformative legislature," unlike the British parliamentary system, which he described as an "arena legislature."[11] Congress, according to Polsby, possesses the "independent capacity, frequently exercised, to mold and transform proposals from whatever source into laws."[12] Such a legislature is best understood by examining its internal structures and processes. In an arena legislature, by contrast, the real power is outside the legislature itself, such as parties, pressure groups, and the social backgrounds of legislators. An interesting and important question is whether Congress is now sufficiently weakened that it has become more of an arena legislature rather than a transformative one.

David R. Mayhew, another scholar who studies Congress, argues that what we now have in America is a presidential system run by executive leadership, with the role of Congress best understood as providing "legitimacy" to presidential leadership.[13] Occasionally Congress may reject a president's initiative but, importantly, nearly all the initiatives come from the president. Congress undertakes very little original action, instead contenting itself to approve, and thereby legitimate, a president's leadership, or not. Again, this falls well short of the Founders' vision that the legislature would be the first of the branches.

Making Congress Function Again

Even when Congress seems inclined to act, however, a host of institutional problems gets in the way. The old order of doing business in Congress—deliberation through committees, debates, amendments—has been replaced by a new metaphor of war. Rather than sending bills through the committee process, the majority leader in the Senate holds a bill in secret until the necessary votes are there to pass it, and then springs it on the Senate for approval. Consequently, when legislation is passed these days, it is often on a party-line vote, with no engagement or involvement by members of the other party. In fact, the primary legislative accomplishment of the Obama administration—the Affordable Care Act—was passed on a party-line vote of Democrats, and the signature bill of the Trump era, tax reform, was enacted on a party-line vote of Republicans. This has become the new normal, with party unity voting increasing from about 60 percent in the 1970s to nearly 90 percent today.[14]

Voters and their political parties do play a key role in this increasing partisanship in Congress. Gone are the days when liberal and moderate Republicans or conservative and moderate Democrats might be involved in building bipartisan coalitions to get things done. Now, thanks to party sorting, Republicans are almost uniformly conservative and Democrats nearly all more liberal. As political scientist Morris Fiorina points out, "[P]arty sorting is the key to understanding our current political turbulence. . . . [E]ach party has become more homogeneous internally and more distinct from the other."[15] Professor Alan I. Abramowitz points out that the US Senate, during the forty years 1969–70 to 2009–10, saw the proportion of Democratic senators classified as moderate fall from 36 percent to 7 percent, and moderate Republicans from 48 percent to 10 percent. Abramowitz concludes that this "rise of ideological polarization [has made] bipartisan cooperation increasingly difficult" and has also had the effect of strengthening the hand of party leaders.[16]

The tools of legislative war used in Congress—the filibuster, the nuclear option, filling the amendment tree—might seem to be the problem, but the underlying cause of the war is far more significant than the weaponry itself. In Congress the minority party has decided its purpose is to obstruct the agenda of the majority party, and the majority party sees its goal as limiting the opportunities for the minority. As political scientist Steven S. Smith has put it, "Leaders are expected to fully exploit the rules in the interest of their parties. The minority is quick to obstruct and the majority is quick to restrict."[17]

The weapons of this legislative war receive most of the attention and, while they can be effective, they sound like frustrating insider baseball to voters. For example, a senator may speak for extended periods of time (filibuster), with Senate rule XXII requiring sixty senators to decide that an issue has been sufficiently debated and vote for cloture. This allows a minority to obstruct the majority by holding the floor and requiring a super-majority vote to move things along. The filibuster and cloture game was rarely played before the 1970s but, especially during the Obama administration, it became routine. Finally, frustrated by Republican filibusters and threats of filibusters, Senate majority leader Harry Reid invoked the "nuclear option," reducing the vote required to end debate on appointees other than Supreme Court justices to a simple majority in 2013. The new Senate majority leader, Mitch McConnell, then led the Senate to require only a simple majority for Supreme Court justices to be approved, allowing the nomination of Neil Gorsuch to be confirmed in 2017.

By now Congress rarely deliberates, which was its original purpose. Beginning in George W. Bush's second term, continuing through the Obama years, and now in the Trump administration, Congress does very little debating and deliberating, instead largely bringing forward bills that one party has the votes to enact. As James Wallner points out in his book *The Death of Deliberation*, "Reasoned deliberation has nearly disappeared in the contemporary Senate as decision-making has gradually migrated from committee hearings and the Senate floor to informal and ad hoc meetings . . . typically held under the auspices of the party leadership and out of public view."[18] Committee chairs, who used to wield considerable power and influence, have effectively been replaced by party leaders. Bipartisanship, civility, respect for, and trust in Congress seem all but lost. Despite repeated calls for Congress to return to "regular order," the combat continues.

It will be difficult, perhaps even impossible, for Congress to reform its way back to greatness. It would seem to be time for another congressional reform act, as was accomplished in 1946 and again in the 1970s. Congress needs to meet more often than Tuesday through Thursday with weeks of recesses, and members need to spend their time in Washington actually legislating, not raising money to run for reelection. More than that, however, it will require greater statesmanship and leadership by its members, such as that exhibited by Senator John McCain when he flew back to Washington from his cancer treatments to vote "no" on repealing and replacing Obamacare precisely because the reform had not been developed in a thorough and bipartisan way. McCain said it was time for the Senate to "return to the correct way of legislating and send the bill back to committee, hold hearings, receive input from both sides of the aisle, heed the recommendations of the nation's governors, and produce a bill that finally delivers health care for the American people." There needs to come a day when this kind of call for bipartisanship and regular order does not come only from so-called maverick leaders.

Then, too, the American voters have a role to play if we are to make Congress great again. Voters should not think about nonpresidential elections as merely "off-year" or "midterm" elections but rather as opportunities to send the kind of leaders to Washington who will make Congress great again. We need fewer party loyalists and more deliberators, less toeing the line and more crossing party lines. Voters should elect some leaders who, as in an earlier day, had a strong institutional commitment to the House or Senate, not just to their own political party. If we cannot make Congress great again, perhaps we can at least make it relevant, possibly even transformative.

Making Congress Deliberative Again

It is necessary, but not sufficient, to make Congress great again. We must also make Congress deliberative again. As we noted earlier, the Senate especially, referred to by former president

James Buchanan as "the greatest deliberative body in the world," hardly deliberates anymore. Party leadership has supplanted the role of once-powerful committee chairs. With party sorting leaving very few moderates, and even fewer liberal Republicans or conservative Democrats, there is little bipartisanship on major issues. Party-line voting is the new normal, with leadership sharply limiting the possibility of hearings, debates, and amendments. As political scientist Barbara Sinclair has written, "The Senate now often appears to be an arena for partisan warriors, with the party teams willing to use all the available procedural and public relations tools without restraint."[19]

Changing an institution such as the US Senate would be difficult under the best of circumstances. Professor Burdett Loomis has observed some of the qualities that make the Senate difficult to change, including its "non-majoritarian, highly individualistic" nature, with its "unique combination of tradition, precedent, and constitutional mandate."[20] A few wonder how much change is truly needed, whether this period of contentiousness and relative inactivity is part of a longer-term and natural cycle in Congress. Congressional expert Nelson Polsby has observed that Congress has periods of unanimity and activity followed by periods of disagreement and stalemate, with the latter lasting, on average, "about twice as long" as the former.[21]

Others argue that the underlying problem is that the country itself is deeply divided about policy and that the warlike atmosphere in Congress reflects the spirit of the people as a whole. Congressional elections, especially for the Senate, have increasingly become national, not only constituting primarily a referendum on the sitting president's policies but also on the policy preferences of the two major political parties. National parties now become heavily engaged in recruiting and funding candidates for Congress. As a consequence, the warlike atmosphere, with candidates taking strong positions on opposite sides of issues, lays the groundwork for a highly partisan Congress following the election. Presidents often overplay their hand after winning an election, pursuing ideas outside the mainstream consensus, again resulting in real policy disagreements. Examples of this would include Bill Clinton pressing for national health care reform immediately following his election, or George W. Bush seeking to privatize Social Security when he won a second term. As scholars David Brady and Craig Volden suggest in their book *Revolving Gridlock*, "The predicament of contemporary politics in America could be relieved by lowering public expectations about what the government is able to achieve, given the diversity of views held by Americans and the complexity of the problems with which the country is faced."[22]

The more conventional view, however, which we share, is that the warlike atmosphere, the lack of deliberation, and the growing dysfunction in Congress are well beyond any normal range of operation. It certainly is both desirable and possible to make Congress deliberative again, but it would require political will on both sides of the aisle to move in that direction. For example, House and Senate leaders could shift power back to committees and committee chairs as part of a return to regular order. Beginning with Tip O'Neill as Speaker of the House (1977–87) and continuing under Speaker Newt Gingrich's Contract with

America (1994), considerable power has been taken from committees and committee chairs and consolidated in the Speaker's office. It became a world of "leadership-controlled agendas, fewer committee staff and reduced procedural power for committee chairs," which, along with other changes, "completed the neutering of the committee begun in 1980."[23]

Prior to his election as Speaker of the House of Representatives in 2010, John Boehner explained how strong congressional committees promote civility by engaging people on both sides to look closely at legislation. Strengthening committees would also, as Boehner pointed out, encourage the formation of bipartisan coalitions along regional or issue-specific lines, rather than on purely partisan party lines.[24] This could be a key first step toward returning Congress to regular order: starting at the committee level, getting buy-in from ranking members, working bills slowly, inviting input from the minority, and developing consensus so that a bill comes to the floor with both majority and some minority support.[25] Unfortunately, though the leadership of both parties has promised this repeatedly, the temptation to hold power and win seems to triumph over improving the process.

Certain rules adjustments, especially in the Senate, could help make the legislative process more deliberative. There is nothing in the Constitution about the filibuster or cloture, so these are only matters of Senate rules. If the Senate wishes to maintain the filibuster—an open question after the exercise of the so-called nuclear option in recent years—it would make sense that the cloture vote requirement be lowered from three-fifths to a simple majority, or even 55 percent of senators present and voting, so as to keep one senator or a small minority from clogging up the legislative process entirely. There could also be certain categories of legislation—the calendar, appropriations, and tax measures, for example—where such obstructionism could be limited.[26] The practice of allowing a single senator to unilaterally place a "hold" on a nomination or other action should be stopped.

Internal reform of rules alone will not be enough to restore deliberation, but it could help. Deeper qualities such as compromise, moderation, bipartisanship, and civility need to be restored in Washington. Compromise, once a foundational approach to legislating, is almost a dirty word these days. Politicians fear that voters will punish them if they give in to the other side. As Jonathan Rauch points out in his essay "Rescuing Compromise," however, polls show that voters actually prefer compromise, especially if it helps "get things done."[27] Congressional factions such as the Tea Party are especially unwilling to compromise, preferring instead to shut down the government if they do not get their way. Voters will need to pressure and reward members of Congress who make reasonable compromise in order to effect good policy.

Moderation also needs to be restored to the vocabulary and practice in Washington. James Madison suggests in *Federalist* No. 37 that moderation is a virtue that needs to be taught, writing with regret "that public measures are rarely investigated with that measure of moderation, which is essential to a just estimate with their real tendency to advance or obstruct the public good." Moderation does not see public policy as war, but rather, as David Brooks wrote, "a voyage with a fractious fleet." It is not an ideology, Brooks continued, "it's a way of coping with the complexity of the world."[28] Unlike warriors, moderates understand that there are often good ideas on various sides of an issue, and seek to bring those together into good public policy.

The goal is to return to the Founders' notion that deliberation by Congress is an important priority and a useful process. Congress was intended both to represent the American people and to process important policy initiatives.[29] It is in the processing that deliberation is so important. We agree with James Wallner when he said that deliberation was intended to educate senators and, by extension, the public on the great choices. The deliberative process was designed not to pass bills quickly but to "preserve individual liberty by checking popular opinion without undermining the republican principles on which the Constitution rested."[30]

Below the Line:
Are the People Polarized and at War?

Today elites of all kinds have taken up the charge that the failures of American democracy are the fault of the people themselves. Some point to low voter turnout as evidence that the American people are laying down on their democratic jobs. Still others blame the wave of selfish and backward populism that elected Donald Trump for the problems with American politics and policy today. Of course, things are far from perfect below the line, but we doubt that the people are the primary cause of problems in our republic, especially the one we have called out: turning public policy from deliberation to war. If you were to listen to the media, you would believe that the people are hopelessly polarized and the cause of the gridlock and warlike atmosphere among political leaders. The success of presidential candidates such as Donald Trump and Bernie Sanders in 2016 shows, in the view of some, that more extreme red and blue camps are growing. Polls showing that Republicans support Donald Trump by large percentages while Democrats oppose him in comparably large numbers are cited as further evidence of the divide. The Pew Research Center has carried on a multiyear project showing how political polarization has grown among Americans.[31]

There is plenty of evidence to the contrary, however. For example, an AP-NORC poll in September 2017 showed a considerable spread of political views among Americans, with "strong Republicans" and "strong Democrats" among the smaller percentages on the scale. While there are so-called red and blue states, when you break them down into counties, there is a lot of hybrid purple on the American political map. It is not at all clear that grassroots polarization is driving polarization and gridlock in Washington.

A better narrative to explain sources of division, according to political scientist Morris Fiorina, is party sorting. The political parties are better sorted in that there are now relatively few liberal or moderate Republicans or conservative or moderate Democrats. However, Fiorina argues that most voters "are not as well sorted as party elites and many voters do not identify with the parties at all."[32] In an interview, Fiorina argues that while the parties are more at odds than ever, "this elite-level polarization hasn't infected most of the American electorate."[33] Ordinary people do not like the party warrior mentality, Fiorina says.

In his classic 1992 book *Why Americans Hate Politics*, E. J. Dionne described the early days of this kind of political sorting and warfare. Dionne argued that politicians went onto the campaign battlefield seeking to divide voters and conquer the election over one hot button social issue or another (abortion, gun control, and the like). But when they got into office, they did nothing about those things, since they were essentially fabricated to win elections. The problem, according to Dionne, is with political elites who want polarization to raise money and win elections, not with the people.

One serious problem that afflicts people below the line is the poor state of civic education in America. The Founders understood that education was a key requirement of a free nation. George Washington, in his first annual message to Congress (1790), said, "Knowledge is in every country that surest basis of happiness." More than that, Washington added, education secures "a free constitution" by teaching people "to know and value their own rights" and to discern when they are threatened and need protection. In fact, Washington and other Founders saw education as of sufficient importance to the republic that he advocated the creation of a national university for its citizens. Alexis de Tocqueville observed that purpose of education in America, writing, "the sum of men's education is directed toward politics."[34] Both Tocqueville and Madison recognized that a republican form of government "presupposes" (as Madison put it in *Federalist* No. 55) that its citizens possess virtues that we would argue are developed through civic education.

Unfortunately, civic education has fallen in disrepair in the American republic of the twenty-first century. In the latest national tests of eighth graders on American history, for example, an embarrassing 18 percent were proficient or above, and only 23 percent were proficient or higher in government. A mere 1 to 2 percent tested as "advanced." A poll of eighteen-year-olds found that 77 percent could not name a senator from their home state and many young people think Judge Judy of television fame is on the US Supreme Court. Increasingly, young people say they believe in socialism, yet further questioning reveals they do not understand what socialism is. It is a scary thought when we contemplate a statement attributed to Abraham Lincoln, "The philosophy of the school room in one generation will be the philosophy of government in the next."

It is nigh on impossible for the republic to function if its citizenry does not understand its rights, privileges, and duties. In fact, a recent study concluded that if the republic is in danger, more and better civic education is an important part of the answer. The study "The Republic Is (Still) at Risk and Civics Is Part of the Solution," by Peter Levine and Kei Kawashimi-Ginsberg (2017),[35] notes that young people are losing faith in democracy and the American system, in part because they do not understand it. Some states are awakening to the problem and are requiring courses and testing in civic education. Several national foundations and funders have begun exploring how to bolster the field. The Ashbrook Center in Ohio has dramatically grown its programs to train and retrain teachers of history and civics to use primary documents in teaching. Jeffrey Rosen, head of the National Constitution Center, argues that civic education is the antidote for the stirring of passions by social media.[36] There are signs of hope, but much remains to be done. Clearly, the filters between the people and their democratic leaders will not function if there is not a clear understanding of the nature of the republic and how it is intended to work.

In particular, citizens need to be educated about the value of filters, including checks and balances and separations of power. There are several initiatives afoot to reduce gridlock by weakening these filters further or eliminating them altogether. One example is the stealth effort to undo the Electoral College by passing the national popular vote bill in state legislatures. This bill, when passed by enough states to total the 270 electoral votes needed to elect a president, brings into play a compact requiring member states to cast their electoral votes for the winner of the national popular vote. Unable to muster the votes to change or eliminate the Electoral College by the proper means of a constitutional amendment, this is an end run around one of the filters established by the Founders. Such efforts need to be thwarted, first by educating the American people about the value of these constitutional filters and cooling mechanisms.

Following along behind better civic education should come greater civic engagement. In the Founders' day, it was assumed that citizens would take part in all manner of town hall meetings and civic deliberations. Today, however, our supersized republic renders that sort of citizen engagement difficult, and it is rarely seen. Tools of public deliberation have evolved in recent years to aid in that process. For example, Professor James Fishkin of Stanford University has developed a deliberative poll that allows a random sample of citizens to come together to study an issue, deliberate on it, and express their preferences to government leaders.[37] The Davenport Institute of Public Leadership and Civic Engagement at Pepperdine University trains government leaders, especially at the local and regional levels, to engage the public.[38] These efforts are useful and should be expanded.

Our argument is that the real problems to be solved are at the line, with our filters, and above the line, among our political leaders. It is at these levels that ordinary Americans, who by and large would like to live out their lives without a lot of politics, hope to find solutions. There is work to be done at every level if we are return American public policy to deliberation and away from the war metaphor, which continues to do real damage to both the processes and outcomes of policy making in our nation's capital.

Conclusion

There is no simple three-point solution to the problems created by making public policy into wars and emergencies. We could propose that leaders in Washington stop doing that and return to deliberation, but we are now so steeped in this model of action, wars, and emergencies—and so far from the Founders' intention of deliberation—that it will require all hands on deck at many levels to address the problems.

We argue that the most productive work could be done at the line, where the filters and cooling mechanisms are clogged and broken. Civic associations need to be more than mere government lobbyists, providing a needed layer of civic participation. Returning power to state and local governments will give federalism a chance to work and reduce the dominant role of federal action, wars, and emergencies. The stranglehold of two political parties and their interest groups over policy can be attacked. We must not, as progressives argue, do away with checks and balances and other filters but instead do just the opposite: make them robust and powerful again.

Above the line, our political leaders need to make Congress great again, clawing back powers it has ceded to the president over time. Starting with war powers and the budget, Congress needs to step up to its proper constitutional role. Congress must also return to regular order and become more deliberative. Restoring the power of committees and committee chairs over that of party leaders is a key part of that. Rules changes can help but, in the main, we need more statesmen and fewer party loyalists in Congress.

Below the line, we need to address the civic education crisis while also increasing civic participation. "We, the people" carry the ultimate burden for the democracy, and we have become lethargic and passive. Civic education, in particular, needs the sort of all-out action plan that has been carried out in recent years for science, technology, engineering, and math (STEM). State governments need to set standards and local school districts need to get serious about teaching civics and government.

As this book was being completed, we saw a ray of hope in a *New York Times* article, "How the Senate Got Its Groove Back."[39] It seems that, amid all the rancor and partisanship, senators are quietly working together on a bipartisan basis to restore the congressional power of the purse and set a budget. It seems so basic, yet Senate majority leader Mitch McConnell acknowledged that it had been fifteen years since this had been done properly. Two powerful leaders on different sides of the aisle—Republican Thad Cochran of Mississippi and Democrat Patrick Leahy of Vermont—had taken some trips together and began to talk about the need for bipartisan leadership. Maybe this small effort and more like it could begin to restore much-needed congressional power, deliberation, and leadership.

Yet there are still more dark clouds than silver linings. If we are unable to work toward bipartisanship and deliberation, and continue to govern by wars and emergencies, the ugly alternative is described by Bill Clinton and James Patterson's fictional president: "Our democracy cannot survive its current downward drift into tribalism, extremism, and seething resentment. . . . The freedoms enshrined in the Bill of Rights and the checks and balances in our Constitution were designed to prevent the self-inflicted wounds we face today. But as our long history reveals, those written words must be applied by people charged with giving life to them in each new era."[40]

The choice is ours.

NOTES

1. *Rasmussen Reports*, "19% Think Federal Government Has Consent of the Governed," April 2014 (http://www.rasmussenreports.com/public_content/politics /general_politics/april_2014/19_think_federal_government_has_consent_of_the _governed).

2. See, e.g., David Schleicher, "All Politics Is National," *The Atlantic*, July 13, 2012. See also, Daniel J. Hopkins, *The Increasingly United States: How and Why American Political Behavior Nationalized* (Chicago: University of Chicago Press, 2018).

3. Alexis de Tocqueville, *Democracy in America*, ed. Harvey C. Mansfield and Delba Winthrop (Chicago: University of Chicago Press, 2000), 489–92.

4. David Davenport and Hanna Skandera, "Civic Associations," in *Never a Matter of Indifference: Sustaining Virtue in a Free Republic*, ed. Peter Berkowitz (Stanford, CA: Hoover Institution Press, 2003), 59–83.

5. See Jeffrey Toobin, "Our Broken Constitution," *The New Yorker*, December 9, 2013.

6. Yuval Levin, "Four Steps for Reviving the First Branch," in *Restoring Congress as the First Branch*, R Street Policy Study No. 50 (January 2016).

7. https://today.yougov.com/topics/politics/articles-reports/2018/04/10/dismal -ratings-congress-though-democrats-are-less-.

8. https://www.politico.com/story/2018/04/02/mitch-mcconnell-republican -senators-frustration-489762?cid=apn.

9. George F. Will, "Congress Insists on Making Itself Irrelevant," *Washington Post*, October 14, 2016.

10. Kevin R. Kosar et al., *Restoring Congress as the First Branch*, R Street Policy Study No. 50 (January 2016).

11. Nelson W. Polsby, "Legislatures," in *Handbook of Political Science*, Vol. 5: *Governmental Institutions and Processes*, eds. Fred I. Greenstein and Nelson W. Polsby (Menlo Park, CA: Addison-Wesley Publishing Co., 1975).

12. Ibid., 277.

13. David B. Mayhew, *Congress: The Imprint of Congress* (New Haven, CT: Yale University Press, 2017).

14. Logan Dancey and Geoffrey Sheagley, "Partisanship and Perceptions of Party-Line Voting in Congress," *Political Research Quarterly* 7 (2017): 32–45.

15. Morris P. Fiorina, *Unstable Majorities* (Stanford, CA: Hoover Institution Press, 2017), 15.

16. Alan I. Abramowitz, "U.S. Senate Elections in a Polarized Era," in *The U.S. Senate: From Deliberation to Dysfunction*, ed. Burdett A. Loomis (Washington, DC: CQ Press, 2012), 28.

17. Steven S. Smith, "The Senate Syndrome," in *The U.S. Senate*, 132.

18. James I. Wallner, *The Death of Deliberation* (Boulder, CO: Lexington Books, 2013), 134.

19. Barbara Sinclair, "Senate Parties and Party Leadership, 1960–2010," in *The U.S. Senate.*

20. Loomis, ed., *The U.S. Senate,* 3.

21. Nelson Polsby, *How Congress Evolves* (New York: Oxford University Press, 2004), 146–47.

22. David W. Brady and Craig Volden, *Revolving Gridlock* (Boulder, CO: Westview Press, 2006), 208.

23. Michael Strand, Michael S. Johnson, and Jerome F. Climer, *Surviving Inside Congress* (Washington, DC: The Congressional Institute, 2017), 353.

24. Ibid., 375.

25. Ibid., 379.

26. Sinclair, "Senate Parties and Party Leadership," 152–53.

27. Jonathan Rauch, "Rescuing Compromise," *National Affairs* (Fall 2013).

28. David Brooks, "What Moderates Believe," *New York Times*, August 22, 2017.

29. Polsby, *How Congress Evolves*, 146.

30. Wallner, *The Death of Deliberation*, 134.

31. See http://www.pewresearch.org/topics/political-polarization/.

32. Ibid.

33. Jeff Stein, "Most Experts Think America Is More Polarized Than Ever. This Stanford Professor Disagrees," *Vox*, November 1, 2016.

34. Tocqueville, *Democracy in America*, 291–92.

35. http://www.civxsummit.org/documents/v1/SummitWhitePaper.pdf.

36. Taylor Lorenz, "James Madison Would Be Horrified by a Tweeting President," *The Atlantic*, June 25, 2018.

37. See James S. Fishkin, *Democracy When the People Are Thinking* (Oxford, UK: Oxford University Press, 2018).

38. See https://publicpolicy.pepperdine.edu/davenport-institute/.

39. Carl Hulse, "How the Senate Got Its Groove Back," *New York Times*, August 19, 2018.

40. Bill Clinton and James Patterson, *The President Is Missing* (New York: Little, Brown and Co., 2018), 504.

About the Authors

David Davenport and Gordon Lloyd are the coauthors of two previous books: *The New Deal and Modern American Conservatism: A Defining Rivalry* (2013) and *Rugged Individualism: Dead or Alive?* (2017). In addition, they have coauthored a number of essays and op/eds in the *San Francisco Chronicle* and elsewhere.

David Davenport is a research fellow at the Hoover Institution at Stanford University, where he also served as counselor to the director and director of Washington, DC programs. He previously served as president of Pepperdine University, where he was also a professor of law and public policy. He is a regular columnist for the *Washington Examiner*, and has previously been a columnist for *Forbes.com*, the *San Francisco Chronicle* and Scripps Howard News Service. He is also a contributing editor to Townhall.com and delivers regular radio commentaries on the Salem Radio Network.

Gordon Lloyd is a senior fellow at the Ashbrook Center and the Dockson Professor Emeritus of Public Policy at Pepperdine University. He is coauthor of three books on the American founding and is editor of James Madison's *Debates in the Federal Convention of 1787*. He is also the creator of four websites on the creation and ratification of the Constitution and the Bill of Rights. He serves on the National Advisory Council for the Walter and Lenore Annenberg Presidential Learning Center through the Ronald Reagan Presidential Foundation.

Index

above the line, 123–24, 128, 133–34, 153–54
Abramowitz, Alan I., 140
action, 9, 76
  action now and, 10–11, 18, 21, 25–26, 34–35, 47, 57, 85–86
  call for, 3
  emergency and, 6
administrative state, 27, 138
Affordable Care Act, 86, 88, 122, 140, 143
Afghanistan, war in, 71
Agriculture Adjustment Act, 38, 42–43
A.L.A. Schechter Poultry Corp. v. United States (1935), 43
All Things to All Men (Hodgson), 40, 54n26
America
  Founders of, 3, 6, 21–23
  under siege, 17
  as world policeman, 5
American conservatism, 48
American exceptionalism, 2, 18
American individualism, myth of, 27
"American Individualism" (Hoover), 2
American Political Science Review, 23n4
American republic
  divided line and, 22, 123–25
  size of, 126
American Revolution, 97, 113
American western frontier, 27
Annual Review of Political Science, 85
Antifederalists, 102–4, 110, 128
Articles of Confederation, 98, 101

Athenian democracy, 96
Authorization for Use of Military Force (AUMF), 71, 82, 84–85

Banking and Currency Committee, 38
Beard, Charles, 27
below the line, 22, 148–53
Bessette, Joseph M., 113, 119n4
bicameral legislature, 99, 106–08
Bill of Rights, 100–101, 105, 155
bipartisanship, 96–97, 155
Boehner, John, 146
border wall, 68
Bowling Alone (Putnam), 129
Brady, David, 145
brain trust, 26
Britten, Fred, 43
Brooks, David, 147–48
Buchanan, James, 144–45
Buchanan, Pat, 60
bully pulpit, 74
Bureau of the Budget, 9, 45
Bush, George W., 12
  executive orders of, 35
  executive power increased by, 82–83
  No Child Left Behind and, 87, 131
  war on terror and, 70–71, 81–86
  as wartime president, 81–82

California, 126
campaign finance reform, 126
Carey, George W., 36, 54n15, 137
Caro, Robert, 59–60, 78
Carson, Ben, 67–68

Carter, Jimmy, 10, 12, 68–70
checks and balances, 41–42, 94, 96, 108,
    115, 118, 154–55
civic associations, 129–30, 154
civic education, 150–52, 154
Civilian Conservation Corps, 35
Clapper, Raymond, 40, 54n27
Clinton, Bill, 6, 23n2, 155
    healthcare reform by, 145
    national emergencies and, 73
    war on drugs and, 66
Cochran, Thad, 155
Cohen, Adam, 48, 53n2, 53n8
cold war, 5
Columbia University, 26
Comprehensive Crime Control Act
    (1984), 63
compromise, 96–97, 147
Congress
    amendment process of, 116
    approval rating of, 135
    as arena legislature, 139
    bicameral legislature of, 99, 106–08
    bipartisanship lack of, 140–43
    committee chairs in, 142, 144–46
    declaration of war and, 9–10, 136
    deliberation, lack of, 18, 142
    as dysfunctional, 135
    elections to, 144–45
    emergency jobs, creation of, 40
    as extension of Roosevelt, F.,
        presidency, 37–38
    filibuster and, 141
    as first branch, 47, 96, 135, 139
    holding bill in secret, 140
    making deliberative again, 143–48
    making functional again, 139–43
    minority party as obstructionist, 141
    national emergencies, review by, 17, 74
    power expelling of, 137
    power loss of, 135–39
    power of purse by, 17, 137
    presidential leadership over, 39

Roosevelt, F., and, 37–40
    shifting power from, 16–17, 25, 47–48,
        135–36
    special session of, 39
    states of emergency, review by, 17
    as transformative legislature, 138–39
    warlike atmosphere in, 144
Congress: The Electoral Connection
    (Mayhew), 24n11
Constitution
    amendment process of, 116
    Article I of, 106, 136
    barriers of, 41–44
    Bill of Rights of, 100–101, 105, 155
    checks and balances of, 41–42, 94, 96,
        108, 115, 118, 154–55
    declaration of war and, 9–10
    elections and, 106, 109–10
    First Amendment to, 127
    Fourteenth Amendment to, 131
    independent judiciary of, 107
    as layman's document, 42
    majority faction and, 113–14
    national emergencies and, 72
    150th anniversary of, 41–42
    ratification of, 102–5
    ratifying conventions for, 97–102
    Roosevelt, F., on, 32, 41–44
    separation of powers of, 41–44, 94, 96,
        107–8, 115, 118
    Seventeenth Amendment to, 112
    signing of, 102
    slavery and, 99–100
    state control and, 13–14
    Tenth Amendment to, 131
    Wilson, W., on, 28
constitutional barriers, removal of,
    41–44, 58
Constitutional Convention, 97–102, 128
Constitutional Dictatorship, 39, 54n24
Constitutional Morality and the Rise of
    Quasi-Law (Frohnen and Carey),
    36, 54n15, 137

Contract with America, 145–46
Coolidge, Calvin, 29
Corwin, Edward, 85
Council of Economic Advisers, 23n1
Council of Revision, 99
The Crusade Years (Hoover), 51
culture wars, 14

Davenport, David, 23n1
The Death of Deliberation (Wallner), 142
Declaration of Independence, 93, 108–9
declaration of war, 9–10
deliberation
  Congress and, 18, 142
  for Constitutional amendment
    process, 116
  Constitutional Convention and,
    97–102, 128
  deliberative poll for, 153
  depravity and, 117–18
  devaluation of, 57
  for development of public policy, 12
  education of Senators by, 148
  emergencies and, 114
  enemies of, 111–15
  enlightened consent of the governed
    and, 108–11
  The Federalist Papers and, 97, 102–5,
    128
  filtered democracy and, 124–33, 152,
    154
  force and fraud and, 116
  Founders, intention of, 3, 6, 116–17,
    148, 153–54
  future of, 115–18
  government of, 94–97
  hurry opposed to, 104, 111
  indoors, 97–102
  as largely gone, 121
  majority faction and, 113–14
  moderation and, 111–12
  New England town meetings
    and, 108

out of doors, 102–5
passions and, 112–13
purpose of, 108–11
reason and, 112–13
rejection of, 116–17
return to, 153
structures for, 105–8
time for, 6
tools for, 153
virtue and, 117–18
war and action replaced by, 76
deliberative poll, 153
democracy, 22–23
Democracy in America (de Tocqueville),
  124–25
The Democratic Civilization (Lipson),
  115, 119n5
Department of Energy, 69
Department of Health, Education, and
  Welfare, 52–53
Department of Housing and Urban
  Development, 78
Department of Justice, 62
Department of Transportation, 78
Dewey, John, 50
Dionne, E. J., 150
direct democracy, 132
divided line, 22, 123–25
domestic wars, 11–12, 24n10, 58–71, 121
  administration departments spanned
    by, 16
  conclusions of, 14
  cost of, 16–17
  culture wars and, 14
  declaration of war on, 9–10
  declared by presidents, 16–17
  deliberation and, 15–16
  effects of, 74–76
  as extension of federal powers, 74–75
  hyperpartisanship and, 86–88
  as marketing campaign, 15
  as never-ending, 14, 16
  oversimplification and, 14–15

domestic wars (*continued*)
  as rarely won, 61
  rhetorical base for, 30–33
  spending authorization of, 17–18
draining the swamp, 8, 134
drones, 84
drug treatment, 66–67, 76
Duncan, Jonathan, 6–7
Dust Bowl, 1
dysfunction in Washington, 133–34

The Economist, 11
economy, federal regulation of, 46
Ehrlichman, John, 81
Einstein, Albert, 122
Eisenhower, Dwight, 52–53, 60
elections, 106, 109–10, 126
Electoral College, 132, 152
Elkins, Jeremy, 9, 23n5
Elks Clubs, 129
Emanuel, Rahm, 25
emergency powers, 72–74
energy crisis (1977), 68–70
enlightened consent of governed,
  108–11
Environmental Protection Agency, 80
Executive Office of the President, 35, 45
executive orders, 30–36, 80, 88, 122,
  137–38
Executive Reorganization Act, 45
expert administrators, 27–28

fake news, 127
The FDR Years (Leuchtenburg), 31–32,
  39, 53n6
fear itself, 3, 26, 30
*Fear Itself: The New Deal and the
  Origins of Our Time* (Katznelson),
  38–39, 54n21
federal budget, 29, 45
federal government
  oversight by, 49
  social injustice and, 50

  transformation of, 47
Federalist No. 1 (Hamilton), 103
Federalist No. 9 (Hamilton), 106
Federalist No. 10 (Madison), 107, 113–14,
  125, 128
Federalist No. 14 (Madison), 94, 107
Federalist No. 22 (Hamilton), 104, 109
Federalist No. 37 (Madison), 95, 111, 147
Federalist No. 38 (Madison), 104
Federalist No. 41 (Madison), 113
Federalist No. 42 (Madison), 111–12
Federalist No. 45 (Madison), 114
Federalist No. 49 (Madison), 113
Federalist No. 51 (Madison), 135
Federalist No. 55 (Madison), 151
Federalist No. 58 (Madison), 137
Federalist No. 62 (Madison), 112
Federalist No. 63 (Madison), 95, 103
Federalist No. 70 (Hamilton), 104–5, 111
Federalist No. 78 (Hamilton), 135–36
The Federalist Papers, 97, 102–5, 128
Federalists, 102–4, 110, 128
Ferguson, Missouri, 64
The Fierce Urgency of Now (Zelizer), 79
filibuster, 141, 146–47
filtered democracy, 125–33, 152, 154
Fiorina, Morris, 149–50
fireside chats, 9, 30, 32, 43–44, 47
First Amendment of Constitution, 127
Fishkin, James, 153
force, fraud and, 116
forgotten man, 30, 50
Forman, James, 64
Founders, 41, 47
  deliberative approach of, 3, 6, 116–17,
    148, 153–54
  on education, 150
  filtered democracy and, 125–33,
    152–54
  government of deliberation by, 94–97
  public good and, 95, 111, 117
Fourteenth Amendment of
  Constitution, 131

Fox News, 127
Franklin, Benjamin, 22–23, 101
Freedom from Fear (Kennedy, D.), 37, 54n16
Freedom of Information Act, 127
freedom of the press, 127
Frohnen, Bruce P., 36, 54n15, 137
frontier thesis, 27

Garland, David, 66
Geneva conventions, 82
gerrymandering, 126
Gingrich, Newt, 145–46
Glass, Carter, 34
Goldwater, Barry, 61
Gordon, Rebecca, 24n10
Gorham, Nathaniel, 97
Gorsuch, Neil, 142
Governing Through Crime (Simon), 64–65
government action, by Roosevelt, F., 18, 21, 25–26
government gridlock, 86–88
great communicator, 9
Great Depression
    action for, 3, 9, 21, 25
    executive orders and, 33–36
    unemployment in, 26
    war metaphor since, 8
    war-like campaign against, 13
Great Society, 10, 13, 48
    Nixon and, 60
    revolution of, 77–79
Guantánamo Bay, 84

Haldeman, H. R., 81
Hamilton, Alexander, 95, 104–7, 109, 111
Hamilton Plan, 98
Harding, Warren G., 28–29
Hartmann-Mahmud, Lori, 15–16
Healy, Gene, 83
Henry, Patrick, 102
Hitler, Adolph, 1

Hodgson, Godfrey, 40, 54n26
Hoover, Herbert
    on federal government powers, 33
    on national bank holiday, 34
    Roosevelt, F., opposed by, 51–52
    rugged individualism and, 2, 29, 33
hot button issues, 150
"How the Senate Got Its Groove Back" (Hulse), 155, 157n39
Howell, William G., 85
Hulse, Carl, 155, 157n39
hyperpartisanship, 86–88

Ickes, Harold, 46, 50
impeachment, 106
imperial presidency, 79–81
incarceration rate, 67, 75
independent judiciary, 107
individual liberty, 50–51
internet, 132
interstate highway system, 52
ISIS, 136
Islamic State, 71
Issues on My Mind (Shultz), 67

Jackson, Robert, 73
James, William, 69–70
Jefferson, Thomas, 94, 98, 112
Johnson, Lyndon, 6, 8, 53
    cabinet departments and, 78
    Congressional power and, 78–79
    Great Society of, 10, 13, 48, 60, 77–79
    presidential power and, 14
    State of the Union message of (1964), 10, 15, 58, 77–78
    The Treatment and, 79
    war on poverty and, 13, 16, 58
    as wartime president, 77
Johnson, Mark, 8, 15
Judge Judy, 151

Katznelson, Ira, 38–39, 48, 54n21
Kawashimi-Ginsberg, Kei, 151

Index

Kendall, Willmoore, 110
Kennedy, David, 37, 54n16
Kennedy, John, (R-LA), 135
Kennedy, John F.
  legacy of, 13, 59
  New Frontier and, 18, 53
  television and, 9
  on war on poverty, 59
Kingston, Jack, 136
Kosar, Kevin R., 138

Lakoff, George, 8, 15, 23n3
Lau, Richard R., 8
Law Enforcement Assistance Act
  (1965), 61
lawyers, 127–28
Leahy, Patrick, 67, 155
Leuchtenburg, William H., 31–32, 39,
  53n6
Levin, Yuval, 134
Levine, Peter, 151
Lincoln, Abraham, 151
Lindley, Ernest, 44, 53n9, 54n15
Lipson, Leslie, 115, 119n5
living constitution, 41
Loomis, Burdett, 144

Madison, James, 21, 84, 95, 97, 99,
  107, 111, 113–14, 118, 125, 128, 135,
  137, 147
mandatory sentences, 67
Mayhew, David R., 24n11
McCain, John, 142–43
McClay, Wilfred, 70
McConnell, Mitch, 99
"The Meaning and Measure of Policy
  Metaphors" (Schlesinger, M., and
  Lau), 23n4
media, 132, 149
melting pot, 7
Metaphors We Live By (Lakoff and
  Johnson, M.), 8, 15
metaphysical world, 123–24

The Mild Voice of Reason (Bessette), 113,
  119n4
Mileur, Jerome, 48, 54n37, 55n41
Milkis, Sidney M., 47–48, 54n37, 55n41
"The Model of War" (Elkins), 23n5
moderation, 147–48
MSNBC, 127
mudslinging, 8

The Nation, 24n10
National Affairs, 134
national bank holidays, 26, 34
National Constitution Center, 105, 152
national emergencies
  Congress review of, 17, 74
  constant, 5
  Constitution and, 72
  current number of, 5, 17, 72–73, 121
  deliberation replaced by, 6
  National Emergencies Act and, 72–73
  thirty-ninth consecutive year of, 72
  war as, 11
National Emergencies Act (NEA),
  72–73
National Industrial Recovery Act
  (NIRA), 31, 36, 38, 43
national popular vote, 132, 152
National Security Agency, 84
NEA. *See* National Emergencies Act
New Deal, 1
  as American French Revolution, 2,
  25, 48
  constitutionality of, 43
  executive orders and, 30–33
  force and fraud and, 116
  Great Depression emergency of, 21, 25
  policies of, 10
  postwar era and, 52–53
  progressive path to, 26–28
  war rhetoric and, 30–33
*The New Deal and Modern American
  Conservatism* (Davenport and
  Lloyd), 1–2

The New Deal and the Triumph of Liberalism (Milkis and Mileur), 54n37
The New Democracy (Ickes), 46
New England town meetings, 108
New Frontier, 18, 52
New Jersey Plan, 98–99
New York Times, 35, 69, 155
NGO. *See* nongovernmental organizations
9/11, 12, 70, 81–82
NIRA. *See* National Industrial Recovery Act
Nixon, Richard, 5, 10, 62
    Environmental Protection Agency created by, 80
    executive orders by, 80
    Great Society programs and, 60
    imperial presidency of, 79–81
    power and, 14
    on presidential candidacy, 87
    resignation of, 81
    Vietnam War and, 79
    wage and price controls by, 80
    war on cancer and, 80
    on war on drugs, 65–66
    on War on Poverty, 80
    War Powers Act veto by, 79–80
    as wartime president, 77
    Watergate and, 81
No Child Left Behind, 87, 131
nongovernmental organizations (NGO), 130
Nothing to Fear (Cohen), 53n2
nuclear option, 86, 141, 146

Obama, Barack, 25
    Affordable Care Act by, 86, 88, 122, 140, 143
    drones, use of, 84
    environmental agenda and, 13
    executive orders by, 35, 88, 137–38
    Guantánamo Bay and, 84
    health care and, 131

    National Security Agency and, 84
    New New Deal and, 51–52
    Paris Agreement on climate change and, 138
    as post-partisan politician, 87–88
    on war on terror, 83–84
Obamacare. *See* Affordable Care Act
Office of Law Enforcement Assistance, 62
Office of Management and Budget, 137
Omnibus Safe Streets and Crime Control Act (1968), 62
O'Neill, P. ("Tip"), 145
opioids, 68
outcome politics, 133

Paris Agreement on climate change, 138
parliamentary system, 40, 132, 138–39
party sorting, 149–50
party-line votes, 19–20, 86, 88, 96, 110, 122, 140, 144
Patterson, James, 6, 23n2, 155
Paul, Rand, 67
Pelosi, Nancy, 99
personal liberty, 117
Pfiftner, James, 83
physical world, 123–24
Plato, 21–22, 123
polarization, 122–23, 148–49
policy prescriptions, 11
political parties, 128–29
political spoils, 27–28
Political Theory, 23n5
Politico, 135
Polsby, Nelson, 138–39, 144
pork barrel politics, 8
presidency
    imperial, 79–81
    modern, 44–49, 116
    power of, 13–14
    shifting power to, 16–17, 22, 25
    as true political leader, 47

Index

The President is Missing (Clinton and
    Patterson), 6, 155
Progressive Party, 27–29, 40
Prospero, 11, 23n6
public good, 95, 111, 117
public policy, 11–12
Putnam, Robert, 129

Al-Qaeda, 70

Raisin Administrative Committee, 52
ratifying conventions, 97–102
Rauch, Jonathan, 147
Rauchway, Eric, 35, 53n11
Reagan, Ronald, 9
    city on a hill and, 18
    on consent of the governed, 110
    war on crime and, 63
    on War on Poverty, 60
Reid, Harry, 141
representative government, 22–23
The Republic (Plato), 21, 123
"The Republic Is (Still) at Risk and
    Civics Is Part of the Solution"
    (Levine and Kawashimi-
    Ginsberg), 151
"Rescuing Compromise" (Rauch), 147
"Resentment Against the Supreme
    Court" (Clapper), 40, 54n27
return to normalcy, 28–30, 114
Review of Reviews, 40, 54n27
Revolving Gridlock (Brady and
    Volden), 145
Robert's Rules of Order, 97
Roosevelt, Franklin D.
    action now and, 10–11, 18, 21, 25–26,
        34–35, 47, 57, 85–86
    brain trust of, 26
    as chief legislator, 39
    Commonwealth speech of, 46
    Congress and, 37–40
    on Constitution, 32, 41–44
    crisis waste of, 25
    fireside chats by, 9, 30, 32, 43–44, 47

first inaugural address by, 2–3, 10
forgotten man and, 30, 50
government action and, 18, 21, 25–26
Great Depression and, 3, 8, 9, 13, 21,
    25, 26, 33–36
Hoover opposed to, 51–52
as master communicator, 30
modern presidency and, 44–49
national bank holiday and, 34
New Deal and, 1, 2, 10, 21, 25, 26–28,
    30–33, 43, 48, 52–53, 116
power and, 14
second inaugural address by, 49–51
on social justice, 50
State of the Union message by, 40
on Supreme Court, 43–44
veto power of, 39
war rhetoric of, 30–33
Roosevelt, Theodore, 9, 27
Rosen, Jeffrey, 105, 152
Rossiter, Clinton, 39, 48–49, 54n24, 85
Rove, Karl, 87
rugged individualism, 2, 27, 29, 33,
    46, 50
Rugged Individualism: Dead or Alive?
    (Davenport and Lloyd), 1–2

salad bowl, 7
Sanders, Bernie, 149
Schlesinger, Arthur, 37–38, 54n17,
    83, 85
Schlesinger, Mark, 8
Schultz, George, 67
science, technology, engineering and
    math (STEM), 155
Senate
    as arena for partisan warriors, 144
    bipartisanship lack of, 144
    committee chairs of, 142, 144
    deliberation and, 121–22
    highly individualistic nature of, 144
    as moderating chamber, 112
    nuclear option of, 86, 141, 146
    party leaders of, 142, 144

party-line voting in, 19–20, 86, 88, 96, 110, 122, 140, 144
  Rule XXII and, 141
  Seventeenth Amendment and, 112
  as world's greatest deliberative body, 143–44
Senate Rule XXII, 141
separations of power, 41–44, 94, 96, 107–8, 115, 118
Sessions, Jeff, 68
Seventeenth Amendment of Constitution, 112
Simon, Jonathan, 64–65
Sinclair, Barbara, 144
singleness of purpose, 11
Skandera, Hanna, 129–30
slavery, 99–100
Smith, Hedrick, 69
Smith, Steven S., 141
social justice, 50
social media, 127, 132
Social Security, 145
socialism, 151
Sorenson, Ted, 59
Speaker of House, 145–46
speed limits, 131
Stanford University, 69–70, 153
State of the Union message (1936), 40
State of the Union message (1964), 10, 15, 58, 77–78
State of the Union message (1970), 62
State of the Union message (1988), 60
STEM. *See* science, technology, engineering and math
Supreme Court, 36, 49
  Judge Judy on, 151
  judicial review by, 99
  nominees to, 86, 141–42
  raisins and, 52
  Roosevelt, F., criticism of, 43–44
Syria, 136

tariffs, 138
Tea Party, 147

Tenth Amendment of Constitution, 131
think tanks, 130
Thinking About Crime (Wilson, J.), 63
Time magazine, 42–43
de Tocqueville, Alexis, 124–25, 129, 150–51
Tonkin Gulf resolution, 77
top two primary voting, 126
trade war, 5
Trading with the Enemy Act (1917), 34
treaties, 137–38
Truman, Harry, 52, 73
Trump, Donald
  Authorization for Use of Military Force and, 85
  campaign cap of, 134
  courts and, 121
  on draining the swamp, 8, 134
  electoral success of, 149
  executive power and, 85
  fake news and, 127
  Guantánamo Bay and, 84
  Obama legacy overturned by, 88, 91n58
  revolving door cabinet of, 138
  selfish populism and, 148
  tariff policies of, 138
  tax reform by, 86
  tweets of, 9, 119n2, 138
  on war on drugs, 68
Tugwell, Rexford, 26
Turner, Frederick Jackson, 27
tweets, 9, 119n2, 138

unemployment rate, 26
United States v. Butler (1936), 43

veto power, 39, 99
Vietnam War, 76, 79
  as Johnson's war, 77
  law enforcement weapons from, 63
  war on crime and, 70
Virginia Plan, 98–99
Virginia Ratifying Convention, 97

Volden, Craig, 145
voting reform, 126

Wallner, James, 142, 148
war metaphor, 7–13, 121, 153–54
  alternatives to, 15–16
  policy development and, 16
  problems with, 14–18
  winning of, 18–20
war on cancer, 80
war on crime, 10, 61, 65, 78
  failure of, 63–64
  militarization of, 64, 75
  Nixon and, 62, 80
war on drugs, 5, 10
  border wall and, 68
  Clinton and, 66
  incarceration rate and, 67, 75
  as losing battle, 67
  mandatory sentences and, 67
  money for, 5, 66
  Nixon on, 65–66
  nonviolent offenders and, 67–68
  opioids and, 68
  treatment, prevention and, 66–67, 76
War on Poverty, 5–6, 9–10, 13, 23n1,
    58, 77–78, 89n8
  continuing of, 16
  cost of, 60
  development of, 15
  Eisenhower on, 60
  Kennedy, J. F., on, 59
  Nixon and, 80
  Reagan on, 60
  small pilot projects for, 59
war on terror, 3, 5, 12, 76, 81–86
  in Afghanistan, 71

Bush and, 70–71, 81–86
  civil rights and, 75
  countries involved in, 70
  Geneva conventions and, 82
  homeland surveillance and, 82
  on Islamic State, 71
  on Al-Qaeda, 70
war powers, leveraging of, 76–86
War Powers Act (1973), 77, 79–80
Wartime Overreaction Theory, 64
Washington, George, 23, 112, 150
Washington Examiner, 23n1
Watergate, 81
wedge issues, 7–8
Why Americans Hate Politics
    (Dionne), 150
Wickenden, Elizabeth, 59
Will, George, 137
Wilson, James Q., 63
Wilson, Woodrow
  administrative state and, 27–28,
    53n3–4
  on Constitution, 28
  executive orders of, 35
World War I, 13
  federal government power during,
    28, 31–32
  return to normalcy after, 28–30, 114
  Roosevelt, F., on, 31
  statutes from, 34–35
World War II, 32, 51, 82, 114

Yoo, John, 82
Youngstown Sheet & Tube Co. v.
    Sawyer, 73

Zelizer, Julian E., 79